Beyond the Mou

BOOKS BY KENNETH REXROTH

POEMS

The Collected Shorter Poems
The Collected Longer Poems
Sky Sea Birds Trees Earth House Beasts Flowers
New Poems
The Phoenix and the Tortoise

PLAYS

Beyond the Mountains

CRITICISM & ESSAYS

The Alternative Society
American Poetry in the Twentieth Century
Assays
Bird in the Bush
Classics Revisited
Communalism, from the Neolithic to 1900
The Elastic Retort
The Orchid Boat: The Women Poets of China (*with Ling Chung*)
With Eye and Ear

TRANSLATIONS

100 Poems from the Chinese
Love and the Turning Year: *100 More Chinese Poems*
100 French Poems
Poems from the Greek Anthology
100 Poems from the Japanese
100 More Japanese Poems (*forthcoming*)
30 Spanish Poems of Love and Exile
Selected Poems of Pierre Reverdy

AUTOBIOGRAPHY

An Autobiographical Novel

EDITOR

An Anthology of Pre-Literate Poetry
The Continuum Poetry Series

KENNETH REXROTH

Beyond the Mountains

A New Directions Book

ACKNOWLEDGMENT

These plays have appeared in the following periodicals: *The Quarterly Review of Literature, Portfolio, New Directions IX* and *XI,* to which thanks and acknowledgment are due. Much of the work was done on two Guggenheim Fellowships, an honor and aid of which the author is deeply sensible.

Manufactured in the United States of America.
First published clothbound by New Directions in 1951. Published paperbound by City Lights Books in 1966. This edition published as New Directions Paperbook 384 (ISBN: 0-8112-0552-5) in 1974.
Published in Canada by McClelland & Stewart Ltd.

New Directions Books are published for James Laughlin
by New Directions Publishing Corporation
333 Sixth Avenue, New York 10014

FOR MY DAUGHTER, MARY

CONTENTS

AUTHOR'S NOTE

These plays are all concerned, as will be obvious on reading them, with the same root types, the same dramatic figures; with the relation of the person to the world of occurrence—of what might and what does happen. They portray the interaction of varying degrees of overcoming and immersion in the tangle of thought, will, and chance.

The first two plays do not culminate in dramatic resolution or climax; rather an atmosphere is created, a general situation developed, and dramatic realization occurs as a sort of precipitate crystal from the saturated solution of dramatic tensions—not a kind of happening, but a state of being. Iphigenia marches straight to transcendence. Phaedra and Hippolytus achieve transcendence but are destroyed by impurity of intention. In *Hermaios* and *Berenike* all the characters are caught in the web of cause and effect, and the reader will have to judge for himself who achieves transcendence, how, and to what degree.

The general ideas which have guided me in writing these plays are also discussed in my long poems, *A Prolegomenon to a Theodicy, The Phoenix and the Tortoise,* and especially in my recent work, *The Dragon and the Unicorn.* (*New Directions* XII) The plays and *The Dragon and the Unicorn* complement each other and could be read profitably together.

Five crucial lines of *Berenike* can be found in a

somewhat similar form in the play of a contemporary on the same subject. Since I have been working on these plays for ten years, the discovery of this coincidence—something like the sort of thing which happens sometimes in the sciences—tremendously upset me at first. However, I have been assured that there is only a superficial resemblance. Certainly our ideas and purposes in choosing this plot seem to be completely antagonistic.

K. R.

PHAEDRA

PHAEDRA

First Chorus, two people
Second Chorus, four people

Hippolytus
Phaedra
Theseus

The Greek Heroic Age.
Before the palace at Athens.

At the back of the stage, a screen, seven feet high and ten feet wide with a rough black and white sketch of a small, primitive, columned building, of the wooden Doric type postulated in histories of architecture. Along the bottom of this screen is a step about one foot high. At right and left are screens, seven feet high and four feet wide, hinged to the wall or wings, which can be pulled back, on a cord, towards the audience, by members of the Second Chorus.

On the step, at right and left, sit the First Chorus. At right is a young girl, barefoot, dressed only in a single black cloth, tightly wrapped like a sarong—a street prostitute. At left is a fat old man, with shaved head, wrapped in a white cloth, a small brass bowl beside him—a beggar. The First Chorus speak with great

13

dignity and treat the principals with a certain condescension. All business with the principals is done by them, except Hippolytus' last entrance.

The Second Chorus sit, two and two, along the walls on either side, in front of the screens. They are inconspicuously dressed, possibly in long dull blue gowns. They are the musicians, mob, commentators, prop men, and sound effects.

On her entrance Phaedra may be dressed in gauze trousers, jeweled brassiere, heavy jewelled girdle, extremely high heeled slippers, a headdress like a Chinese bride's, a great deal of jewelry, bracelets and anklets— a newsboy's idea of a harem queen. These are all removed for her first dance. Afterwards, she wears the same costume as the prostitute, but without jewels.

Hippolytus wears a white cloth, with his arm and chest bare. The cloth is tied with a cord around his waist, draped over his shoulders, the way Indians are supposed to wear blankets, but somewhat shorter. He is barefoot. This is the same costume as the beggar's.

Theseus is dressed in a simplified version of a light-armed Greek soldier's costume, carries a short sword and a fiddle-shaped shield.

The couch is a stout folding camp bed, covered with a white blanket. The cup is a plain white hemispherical bowl about eight inches in diameter. There should be a set of fragments of a similar cup. The sword is in a plain scabbard, has a cruciform hilt, and looks rather like a child's wooden sword.

There is no curtain. At the beginning the Choruses walk on, take their places, tune their instruments and begin. At the end, players and Choruses rise and file out, in "reverse precedence," as at Mass.

The dances in all these plays should be restrained and formal and very slow. They should under no circumstances resemble the expressionist dance fashionable in America in the Thirties.

The make-up should be as formal as possible, or, much better, the three principals and the First Chorus should wear masks. If masks are used, the corpses should be dummies.

Except for the jewelry, the colors should be exclusively black and white.

The instruments for the music for these plays should include viola, flute, percussion—wood and drums— very little or no metal, and plucked strings—either an Irish harp, a zither, dulcimer or guitar.

I CHORUS
  What hour is this, what day?

  We have seen the eclipsed sun
  Cut by the sea horizon,

The light rush from the gray sand,
The still sea turn black, the sky
Turn black, and the stars come out,
And the wind rise with the dark
With an uncanny rustling
Noise like stiff pleated tissues
Moving with the shadow's edge.

The owls called in the shadow.

We watched from the dark seashore
And the secret icy hair
Of the sun sprang on the sky,
And the ring of the sun's blood.

Behind us all the cocks crowed
In every blackened farmstead,
And every dog cried with fright.

They rose from the sea and sprang
Apart, and all day the sun
Looked as though it had been bled,
All day the black moon followed,
Hidden across the bright sky.
Soon in the red evening
It will hang in the sunset,
Thin as imagination.

II CHORUS

Our country is very sick.
Crops wither and men quarrel.
Something is wrong with our queen.

A city is like a hive—
Evils possess its rulers

And its life becomes deranged.
The life of the people hangs
On the womb they crown with gold.
Men and beasts become sterile
When it sickens and withers.

Nightmares escape from her dreams
And tramp the seeded furrow.

If she does not heal or die
Soon, we will all have perished.

Theseus wanders in Hell
On a fool's errand; his heir
Plays hermit in the forest,
Forsakes a king's duties for
A saint's gelded wantonry.

Life should flow from our rulers—
They rape the queen of the dead,
Couple with ghosts, lie between
The freezing limbs of the moon.

Hippolytus is the worst.

There was no better prince once.

It was a pleasure to see
Him staggering hot with wine,
Under each arm a young girl,
Squirming in her red drawers.

He certainly liked young girls.

Yes, the younger the better.
Every year he deflowered

Half the town's crop of virgins.

That's the duty of a prince,
To open bellies for new
Infant armies to march out.
He's a lucky man who gets
A girl unsealed by a prince,
Their daughters make the best wives,
Their sons the bravest soldiers.

He's changed.

Seeing that leper
Turned his royalty sour.

Was it a leper? I heard
He stepped on a corpse one night
When he was drunk and roaring.

I heard he saw a crazy
Blind, bald, toothless, old woman;
And they told him she was once
Herakles' sweetheart and taught
Him to love in his young days.

Do you see that beggar there,
Sitting on the palace steps?
I think he really scared him.
They say he was a king once.
Theseus took his city,
Killed his children, raped his wife,
And hamstrung all his horses.
Now he idles in the woods,
And lives on nuts and berries,

Sleeps with the moon in summer,
And nests in a temple porch
In the wintertime. They say
Those cropped ears can hear
The foolish words of the dead,
The wise words of the undying.

They are hitching up the chariot.
I guess he is leaving soon.

He didn't stay long this time.

Hippolytus enters.

HIPPOLYTUS
Are the horses ready? Hurry.
I can't get away quick enough.
I feel as though I'm chained with gold
Inside a jewelled prison cell
That gets smaller every hour,
A harem full of manacled
Skeletons and behind the stone
Eyes in the dry skulls of the king's
Councillors—spiders and sowbugs.

I CHORUS
You leave a lot undone.

HIPPOLYTUS
Leave it
To the sick queen and her vapors.
Let my father's politicians
See to the quarrying of stone.

Let them build banks, tombs, whorehouses.
Tell them to convert the palace
Into a pyramid. I'll sleep
In it when I have turned mummy.

I Chorus

In the mountains the wind rustles
The leaves. Deep in the night the deer
Cry out beyond the edge of dreams.

The black queen has married the sun.
All the next fortnight she will grow
Big with the sun's blood inside her.

Hippolytus

Deep in the forested mountains
There is a meadow where a wild
Apple tree grows. For fourteen days
The buds will open one by one
As the moonlight grows in the tree.
The sun's blood will stream from the moon's
Veins into the veins of the tree,
And the mist of vision descend
In perfume and light around me.

I Chorus

They say there was a city there,
Greater than Knossos or Athens.
Ten thousand years ago its walls
Were smashed down, its temples looted,
Its girls' gauze bottoms and spiced breasts
Left splattered on the smoking stone.

Now that tree changes all the dust
Of riot and debauchery
To pride and chastity and peace.

HIPPOLYTUS

Vein and artery are braided
Into the branches of that tree.
It is the cord that feeds my heart
From her pure compassionate heart—
Artemis, who hears the world's cry.

I CHORUS

Your chariot is ready now.

HIPPOLYTUS

Good-by, pesthouse. I only hope
I never have to smell your stink
Of lust and murder anymore.

He goes out.

II CHORUS

They say she is worse, the last
Three days she has refused food.

She is weak now and can scarce
Walk.

Before, she paced her room
Continuously, or called
For her chariot, only
To send it away unused;
Or she rode out aimlessly,

And then returned suddenly,
Forgot what she had gone for;
Or she took the reins herself,
And drove like mad, hair flying,
Lashing the horses, headlong
Nowhere, and then she'd stop short
And stare and fall in a muse.

Sometimes she would spend the day
And night sleeping like a corpse.
Another time her lamp
Would burn all night and we
Would hear her moving around.

She is certainly beautiful.

It is terrible to see
Such beauty destroy itself.

They say it takes two thousand
Years to make beauty like that.

She sat at the loom doing
Nothing. The shuttle fell from
Her hands, or else she flung it
Back and forth between the threads,
Empty.

She called for music,
And then said the sound was like
Hot nails driven in her ears.

For a week she drank thick wine
Day and night. It didn't seem
To affect her, now she won't

Even taste wine; and at last
She has refused to touch food.

They are bringing her outdoors.

She wants to lie in the sun.

Maybe it will do her good.

Phaedra is carried in on a couch.

PHAEDRA
Take me back. You shouldn't have moved me.

I CHORUS
You said you wanted the sunlight.

PHAEDRA
I know. But I don't want it now—
Not that violent animal,
Tearing at my eyelids and bowels.

I CHORUS
Phaedra. The sun will give you strength.

PHAEDRA
I don't want his strength. I've my own.
It is strength that makes these white thighs
Too weak to walk. I have ample
Strength at my spine's black root—
I don't need all his cheap blonde noise.

I CHORUS
Please sit up. Please. Please try to eat.

23

PHAEDRA

Damn you to Hell. Let me alone.
I have more than enough to eat.

I CHORUS

This beautiful, beautiful flesh—
Why do you try to destroy it?

PHAEDRA

Don't worry. It won't be injured.
This stuff is immortal, passing
From dying spirit to spirit.
Wisdom, lust, chastity and war—
All the gods try to destroy it—
But they never will. They themselves
Live on human flesh. You know that.
Or have you everything backwards,
Like all the other buffleheads?
Give me your hand.
Touch my belly.
This is the phoenix' nest. Someday
I shall burn myself up in it,
And walk from the smoke a virgin.
Come back.
Are you afraid of me?
Give me some wine.
It is pretty,
Isn't it? You know my sister
Bathes in it with her black lover.
People that see them go crazy.
"The gold lion watches himself
In the unruffled forest pool.

He is immortal. His image
Is immortal." That is my flesh.
It will never, never, never,
Die.

I CHORUS
Lean back. Let me comb your hair.

PHAEDRA
Give me the mirror.
It drinks me.
It has drunk up the smiles of girls
Ever since Daedalus made it—
Before I was born, in Crete.
That octopus carved on its back
Is fat with all those painted lips
Sucked under in its polished lie,
Drowned with the fleeting, pouting smiles
Of expected kisses frozen
Upon them.
Women made these holes
In space, into the other world.
The inhabitants of that world
Peer and mock at us, grimacing
In the elastic masks of our
Identities.
And memory—
This is memory. All the world,
Everything, falls in here. This thing
Sends its radiant loneliness
Out like a cloud, and draws it back,
And everything with it. It is

The way the thing breathes. Take it
Away.
Apathy. Do you know
What real apathy really is?
Mountains are apathetic, too.
I see the sun on the mountains
Of ice that I have never seen.
Against their apathy I have
Only pain trickling from their cold
Like a waterfall. That water
Flows through endless, immense forests,
Sinuous and sweet, between the pines
Of two thousand years. The rabbit
Drinks, and the weasel, in the night
Of eyes. Young men go naked there.
What did I say?
You know, at night
The air is full of flying knives—
Daylight my brain is the center
Of a mirror without limit.

I Chorus

What is it haunts you? Into what
Cobweb of fire have you fallen?

Phaedra

I didn't ask to be involved.
I never wanted to be here.
O God how I wish I were home—
Back home in the ruined city—
My father killed at the altar
In the heart of the labyrinth—

Nothing left but the broken walls—
The crumbling frescos scrawled with smoke
And the obscenities of Greek
Infantrymen.
I don't want this.
There will never be anything
Like it again. These savages
Will perfect a new savagery.
Once more the art will be refined
Of fanning every appetite
And stifling every desire.
But there will be a difference—
And I shan't be royal priestess.
Do you know that these arms that I
Can hardly lift have held the coiled
Adders of double death like flowers?
This will-less hand has struck the dark
With the double axe of lightning?
And here I am, a pirate's whore.
It's not the change that you might think.
A princess is a kind of whore,
The peasant's gorgeous imagined
Bedfellow. We serve to provide
Insatiable appetites
That keep men busy. If it weren't
For us there'd be no history.
Our emperors find us frigid.
When our empires fall, and we pass,
Raped, to barbarian chieftains,
I suppose they wonder, lying
Against our chilly backs, what all
That getting and spending was for.

Still, we teach them to read and bathe.
Enslaved by blood and freed by lust,
The court ladies of dead Knossos
Become prostitutes in Athens.
But not me. I'll never be freed.
I am the proof of the pudding—
What it was all for—my sister
And I, all that blood nastiness
And ruin. She was abandoned
To a drunken Indian, and I
Am being smothered to death.
I'm hot.
Take these clothes from my body.
This barbarian frippery
Dries up my womb like acid hate.
I wish I were naked in cold
Water. I want to be taken,
Plunged in a freezing cataract,
My flesh burst with monstrous male flesh.
My mother's demoralized womb
Bore me, that first had borne the bull.
Saluting soldiers, and shivering
Peasants and prostrate worshippers—
Their appetites sent them to Hell,
Chasing each other like lewd dogs.
Let them howl. I am escaped clean.
Only love's absolute will fill
The desire they have left with me.
The best do *not* rot away, I
Am where I do not want to be,
Trapped in a net of illusion,
A stranger amongst savages,

But I am not terrified. Do
You hear me? I cannot be touched.
Help me up.
I want to stand up.
Hold me.
Stop that fumbling.
I am
Going to dance.

I CHORUS
Phaedra.

PHAEDRA
Shut your
Mouths and hold me.
I will be all right.
And take off my clothes.
All of them.

They support her as she begins her dance. When she breaks away she staggers, but gains strength rapidly.

I CHORUS
It is the Minotaur dance,
That she danced with her brother,
In the dark on the bloody floor.
The dance of the fire tangle
That rules the knotted bowels,
The dance of the netted sun,
The black sun in the red earth.

II CHORUS
It is a terrible dance

To watch; ordinary folks
Should not look at things like this.

I CHORUS

She taught the king the heron dance—
The rigid erotic hover
Of the male and female virgins—
The labyrinthine procession;
But Theseus will never see her
Dance like this. It is what his dance
Is for; but he will never know.
For ages the Athenians
Will tread those steps that she taught him;
But they will be pointless, headless.
There will be no one at the heart
Of the labyrinth—no one there
To do what she is doing now.

*At the end of the dance she sits down abruptly,
woodenly, and stares straight ahead. The right screen
reveals Hippolytus. He does not speak or move. She
turns her head stiffly and sees him.*

PHAEDRA

The heart steals the lizard's instant.
I am nailed to the wall.

HIPPOLYTUS

I came back. I have lost my sword.

PHAEDRA

I found it. I have it here.

II Chorus

His sword was hidden in her
Bed, in cloth that smells of her.
His face blenches, but he comes
Forward to take it from her.

Phaedra

Why are the hilt and scabbard
Sealed together, the seal stamped
With a five rayed star? I tried
To draw the blade and could not.

Hippolytus

It is my father's sword, which he
Left with me, and I have taken
An oath that it shall not be drawn.
The witch Medea forged it.
It is an heirloom in Athens.
It has been drawn enough. Too much.
He gave a symbol of power;
But I took from him a symbol
Of my responsibility.
I have sworn never to draw it,
And never to be without it.

Phaedra

You spend all your time hunting;
Don't you ever need your sword?

Hippolytus

Do you want to know my secret?
I will tell you. I do not hunt.

That is just a tale to mislead
My father. Have you ever seen
Me bring home game? Have you ever
Seen blood on my spear or arrows?
He thinks I give the venison
Away to beggars and peasants.
Have you ever seen me eat meat?
I tell him I have a surfeit
At the campfire and need a change.
I have vowed never to take life.
I have taken on the penance
For a career of lust and blood.

PHAEDRA

I thought you were devoted
To Artemis the huntress.

HIPPOLYTUS

Artemis the huntress of souls,
The healer and the avenger,
The lady of the moon filled lake.
She is living retribution,
The peace that unties illusion,
Renunciation that gains all,
The myriad breasted virgin,
The mirror that reflects the sun—
Pure in the dark night of the soul.

PHAEDRA

I am amazed. I cannot
Believe it is you speaking.
I have loved and hated you,

And for all the wrong reasons.
I saw and loved your pride, but
I have hated you, thought you
One of these Hellenes, sensate
Till they are insensible.
They're so sure, and plot the moon's
Course with their machinery.
Someday they may discover
It's held in its orbit by
The menstruation of women.
Come here.
Come and take your sword.

II Chorus
  The sword lies in her soft lap.
  As he takes it by the hilt,
  Her hands cling to the scabbard.

Phaedra
  Someday you will draw this sword
  That Artemis seals shut now.
  When you do, you will kill me.

II Chorus
  Hippolytus is afraid
  Of her. He takes the sword, but
  His whole body is trembling.

Phaedra
  Je fonds comme la neige
  Sur les montagnes d'été.

II Chorus
  She spoke in her own language.

Hippolytus has not moved.

Now she weeps violently.

HIPPOLYTUS

What did you say? Why do you cry?
I never hated you. Always
I have pitied you. Certainly
I do not hate you now. Tell me.
What is the matter? I know now
I have not been alone. I can
Tell you now how much I love you.

PHAEDRA

You do not know, as I know,
You can never understand
As I can—I do not weep
For our private misery,
But for the chaos of the world.

HIPPOLYTUS

I do not know what to say. I
Do not think I understand you.
You have a riddle for a heart,
And I am only a young man.
I have been tortured by conflict.
I have tried to find my duty.
I do not know if I have failed.

PHAEDRA

Realization is hard
To recognize. It's like pain

34

In a nerve you've never used—
Like the pains of childbearing.

HIPPOLYTUS

I'm not sure. I believe I'd know.

PHAEDRA

If you saw her, are you sure
You'd recognize Artemis?

II CHORUS

Hippolytus is dead white.
He can hardly move at all.

HIPPOLYTUS

I think I would. I think I have.
I want . . .

PHAEDRA

Do you want me?

HIPPOLYTUS

I want
What you want.

PHAEDRA

No you don't. But I
Will take you. Maybe it is what
I want.

HIPPOLYTUS

I want you to take me.

I Chorus

They are dancing together.
The prince and the young queen dance.
They dance the dance of the world
That they alone rule over.

It is hard for him to dance.
He must follow her swift steps
As she dances on bright air.

On the rock in the sea's waste
The sea eagle lives alone.
She nourishes her children
On the poisonous sea snakes.
She flies in front of the sun,
Two snakes twisting in her claws.
Once a year her husband flies
To her from the land over
The sea. They mate in mid-air.
The sun is at the zenith,
The full moon at the nadir.
The heart hangs in a gold web.
Moonlight streams up through the earth.
The birds have vanished in fire.

The stage is darkened gradually to black out at the climax of their dance—after a brief interval the lights come up to moderate dimness—Hippolytus and Phaedra are gone. The girl sings.

I Chorus

Lie still. Let your mirror lie.
Lover, look not on the rose

Love has shattered in your hair.
Kiss me. Turn and go to sleep.
Lie still. Our youth goes by us
Like dreamless sleep, soft footed
As our heartbeats and as quick.

Phaedra and Hippolytus enter.

II CHORUS

They are coming out.

They look
Like dead people.

The queen moves
As though she had lost her skin.

You think so? I think the prince
Looks as if there was nothing
Inside his skin.

I suppose
Love like that is wonderful.
But I could do without it.

PHAEDRA

Stop. Look at the million stars.
Do you suppose that someday
They will put us in the stars?
And when you rise they will yoke
Bullocks to the sharpened plow,
And when I set, call the ships
From wandering in the islands.
Stop. No more.

Don't kiss me now.
Maybe they'll separate us
With the river of heaven,
And allow us only once
A year, when we lie against
The sun, to come together.
It's likely to be like that.
We will have to pay for this.
Life, like any property,
Is acquired by theft.
My love.

HIPPOLYTUS

I have never known anyone
Like you. I did not know there was
Anything in the world like this.
I can never love you enough.

PHAEDRA

O lover, lover, lover—
I can't call you that enough.
I knew, but I have never
Found it before. I have been—
For all my lust—a king's wife.
That Aphrodite who turns
Men's hearts inside out never
Haunted the bedside during
My scrimmages with Theseus.

HIPPOLYTUS

Hush. Let me forget my father.
Tonight we are going to start
To make ourselves new memories.

PHAEDRA

People have tried that before.
Memory, unhappily,
Is not some wandering ghost
That the mind can dispossess,
But living bone that our acts
Made powerful over us.
I'd like to forget so much—
But I can never forget.
He may return at any time.

HIPPOLYTUS

Impossible. Come back from Hell?
He has broken in his last gate.
This one will stay shut behind him.
He's there to stay. No lovesick girl
Will give him a clue to that maze.

PHAEDRA

I am afraid you do not
Know the vast frivolity
Of the economy of Hell.
Orpheus overturned it
With a song; and Theseus
Never lacks for stratagems.

HIPPOLYTUS

I don't want to hear it. Kiss me.

PHAEDRA

Besides. If we really have
Found the bliss we think we have,

The glamor of it will shine
Even in that cloudy place,
And he will sense its meaning;
Or else our lust will call him home.
One or the other, someday
He will turn up, the kidnapped
Persephone tagging him
Like a frolicking kitten.
The world's destructive children
Dictate their own terms to fate.
It's people like you and me
Fate traps and the Furies haunt.

HIPPOLYTUS

I'm sorry. I can't be worried.
You lie here philosophizing,
And all I can think of is this curve
Of this smooth belly—these dimples
Where this proud back and buttocks join.

PHAEDRA

O my love—
Is that what you are?
I call you that.
I hope you are.
I can't believe it.

HIPPOLYTUS

How can you say that? For ten years—
Since he brought you back from Crete—
I hardly dared to look at you
For fear I would reveal myself.

You have stood by me in his court,
And your perfume swept over me,
And I have been struck blind with it,
And not known what I was doing.
Or the thought of you has stopped me
In some drunken brawl, and my brain
Has been stripped and sprayed with pepper.
Do you think a live man will take
A goddess as love's surrogate,
If he can have mortal female
Flesh in which to clothe his worship?
While her immortality poured
Into me I could forget you.
The rest of the time I could force
Myself to think of you as his
Embodied lust and disaster.
If I'd not forgotten my sword,
I'd be in the mountains tonight,
Drunk with her immortality.
Maybe I'd never have come back.
I think she might have opened to me
Fully, taken me into her,
Merged my will with her turning disc.
It is too late now, and I feel
This has not been an act of will.
It should have been made to happen—
Not just have happened anyhow.

PHAEDRA

Lover.
Do you know what you're
Saying?

Have you found vision
In a trance under a tree?
Or have you found it elsewhere?
I lay completely open
To you. Did you find it then?

HIPPOLYTUS

I think I did. I know I did.

PHAEDRA

You know indeed.
Do you know
I am a monster's sister?
Do you know what vision costs?
We are each of us tied up
In the inside of a glove.
A great pride or a great lust
Can cut the knot and reverse
The glove. There's no other way—
Vision—evisceration.
The pride must be forged so pure
It fits the lust as a sword
Fits the wound as it cuts it.
That sword with the blade sealed shut
Is the sword of perfect pride.
Have you the right to a sealed
Scabbard?

HIPPOLYTUS

Once more I do not know
If I understand you at all.
But I wonder. Are you so sure

You have the power to be the wound
Only an undrawn sword can cut?
I would rather lie under your
Dragging hair and drink your kisses
Than bandy mysteries with you.
I know that I have wanted you
For years, and at last I have you,
And I am going to keep you.
It's my love against your wisdom.

PHAEDRA

My wisdom is not so deep
That you can't understand it.
It is just the end product
Of a hundred sailors' queens
That slept as deep in the bride
Beds of Knossos as they sleep
On the floors of looted tombs.

HIPPOLYTUS

Kiss me. I'll pay you in full.
What do you want? There is nothing
I have that I haven't given.

PHAEDRA

That will you took ten years to
Sharpen, what should you have done
With it once it was perfect?

HIPPOLYTUS

Would I have given it to you?
Is that what you mean? I don't know.
I doubt if you want submission.

PHAEDRA

Want it? Dear child. I can get
Submission from Theseus
Or any blue-eyed sailor.
Those boys you sent to Knossos,
The lovers of the serpent
Priestess who coupled with her
In the room that my brother
Kept drenched with the blood of girls—
Why do you think they were killed
Before they saw the daylight?
I can only be possessed
By an act that is its own
Memory.
You have it wrong—
Your wisdom against my love.
Only the wise can be proud.
Only the imbecile love.

HIPPOLYTUS

There's been a labyrinth too long
Under your feet, and now you have
An inhuman, labyrinthine heart.
I want the ordinary bliss
Of a human woman's body,
Not a wedding with black nothing.

PHAEDRA

You forgot your Artemis.
You would have been her husband,
Dark moon or full.

HIPPOLYTUS
    I can choose.
    I choose the bright hair on your womb.
    I reject these strands of blackness
    You are trying to spin around me
    Like a hungry female spider.

PHAEDRA
    All right. I make the same choice.
    I can take you to a place
    Beyond memory, beyond
    The sound of talkative Greeks.
    There is a place, a crossroads
    In the Italian jungles,
    Where fugitives from burned out
    Troy and Knossos have settled.
    It is a country of wolves,
    A city with a single
    Mud street and cabins of mud
    And sticks; but men of our race,
    My people and your mother's,
    Struggle with oblivion there.
    Thin-lipped men with narrow waists,
    And long narrow faces,
    The wisest men left alive,
    Wiser than Egypt's mummies,
    Drain the marshes and teach the
    Foolish aborigines.
    They'll die out. They're not enough.
    The wilderness is too big.
    A thousand years of rural
    Idiocy may go by.

But their building and teaching
Will last in those savage brains.
And someday they will pay the heirs
Of Theseus in his own coin.
I could make you a king there.
My royalty is holy
There; I am the only one
Left who can perform those rites.
And I could be your wife there,
Not a Greek's elegant whore,
But the sacred wife who lights
The hearth fires of a new race.
And you could draw that sword there
And bathe me for my marriage
In the immortal blood of bulls.

HIPPOLYTUS

I will let my father found states.
I don't even want to head one.
I have no desire to butcher
Bulls just to make men immortal.
I would prefer that history's
Senseless wheel ran down and the wheel
Of man's appetite that wants to
Go on spinning forever, stop.
They are firewheels made by torches
Whirled in the dark.

PHAEDRA

What do you want?

HIPPOLYTUS

You. For the rest, I'll wait and see.

46

Time is a coiled snake, and deadly
If trod upon.

PHAEDRA
That sounds wise.
It's just procrastination.
I can take what I can get?
All right. I take everything.
It's now or never? This now
Is never. Kiss me. Take me.
You can have the power now
To take me beyond return.
But what returns if you do,
Is your responsibility.
Now do you know what I mean?

HIPPOLYTUS
I understand you. I can see
Fire spray from our union and burn
Down the world, and burn us with it.
Let it burn. We are all burning.
This hand burns. Look at the others
That fall like burning leaves, senseless
Through Hell's cold circles forever.
Your eyes are burning, and the stars
They watch burn, and the reflection
Of the stars in your eyes burns too.
Let this fire fall away in fire,
Like water poured into water.

She stands.

PHAEDRA
Stand up.

Give me back your sword.
Drink before you burn. This cup
Is the brain pan of Minos.
In the starlight, the red wine
Is black as blood in a ditch.

As Hippolytus drinks from the cup which she holds up to him, he drops her dress and she draws the sword.

II CHORUS

Look. They are dancing again.

Again? How can they stand it?
Twice in a day would kill me,
And they haven't eaten yet.

If I was Hippolytus,
I would be afraid of her,
Waving that sword and drinking
She might cut someone with it.

They look like crazy people.

Like people that died crazy.

I CHORUS

Surefooted as sleepwalkers,
They dance on the shifting beams
Of doom's unmeasured levers.

The snake stirs in the earth's core.

The sun hangs in the Bull's horns,
Caught in the Hyades' net.
The moon moves from the Bull's loins.

The snake climbs the last mountain.

The double-headed eagle,
The firebird, flies from the fire.

The five planets crown the snake.

Act and power are mirrored
Pictures in each other's eyes.

The snake crawls into the sun.

The torch goes out, the firewheel
Vanishes in the orb of fire.

The sun's seed is drenched with blood.

Worlds bloom in their flaming hair.

An invisible crystal
Hangs where the sun has gone out.

When the climax of the dance is reached they sustain it, perfectly still, for several seconds, and then spring apart, each with one mechanical leap, downstage, Phaedra right, Hippolytus left.

II CHORUS
What is the matter with them?

I CHORUS
They came together like snow
Whirled in a coiling blizzard.
They mingled like falling rain.
They broke like a falling stone.

49

Neither move. The left screen reveals Theseus.
Phaedra runs across the stage with small, swift
dance steps, the cup and sword still in her hand,
presses against his body and looks into his face.

PHAEDRA

The lictors of Hell, are they
Sentient beings, or merely
Automata created
Especially for the purpose?

She runs out, left.

THESEUS

What's the matter with her? Is she drunk?

II CHORUS

He circles away from him,
His eyes are like a wolf's eyes.

His father is astonished.
His feelings are very hurt.

THESEUS

What's the matter with you? Aren't you
Glad to see me? Stop staring at me.
You can be sure that I'm still alive.
I've had a hard trip and I need rest.
They locked me in the bottom dungeons
Of Hell, but their walls are as flimsy
As smoke, and I walked right straight through them.
Persephone wouldn't come with me.
Although she is a living woman,

She is at the mercy of the dead,
And wanders in the devil's prayers.
However, I had a night with her
Before they caught me. She liked it, too.
I was her first real man in six months.
We were the only live things in Hell
Except for a bull that got lost there
Years ago.   They were afraid of it.
When they found out they could not hurt me,
They tried to get the bull to kill me.
I just got on the poor thing's back, rode
Him out through the closed gates, and came home.
I put him in the stable with your
Horses, you want to watch out for him.
I'm the only one he'll let touch him.
He's a sort of relative, in fact
The bull that the queen's mother once loved.

HIPPOLYTUS

The queen has been violated.

THESEUS

What?   What did you say?   Speak distinctly.

HIPPOLYTUS

I have violated your queen.
I have raped your wife.   What are you
Going to do about it?

THESEUS

Nonsense.
What are you talking about? You mean

You gave her comfort in my absence?
Look, my boy, I am a man of the world.
What do you think I thought would happen?
Do you think that I thought that I could leave
A passionate woman to the care
Of a hot-blooded young sport like you,
And nothing happen? You are my son.
I'd be ashamed if nothing happened.
We were never happy. I never pleased her.
She wanted something I haven't got.
I planned it this way. If I hadn't—
I'd have sent you to the provinces,
And left her in the care of eunuchs,
I'm glad it turned out well. I hope
You give her pleasure and me grandchildren.
If you'd both like, you can have Crete
For your province. Restore the country.
Well? Speak up. Stop that foolish staring.

HIPPOLYTUS

You infamous, infamous man.
I don't wonder Hell spewed you out.
You're a walking Hell of your own.
You have destroyed a dozen wives,
And all your children, and cities
Full of other men, and their wives
And children, the poems of poets,
The visions of artists, the dreams
Of the wise, you destroy them all.
You think there's nothing you can't smash.
You can't smash me. I defy you.
I am where your power ends. Here.

Me. Do you hear me? I smash you.
Let me go. Let me out of here.

He goes out, right.

THESEUS
Fiddlesticks. He will get over that.
He won't be able to keep away
From her if she gets him that excited.
She never had that effect on me.
If I had been better educated,
And had better manners, and a stock
Of high flown talk . . . I've had a hard life.
I'm not young. His mother was my type.
They'll make a fine pair—like his mother
And I did once, but not so brawny.
Where is the queen? Go and bring her back.

*The girl goes out, left. The beggar points as she
pushes out the screen and reveals Phaedra, standing
against the wall, dead, covered with blood from the
waist down.*

I CHORUS
She is dead.

A few moments
Ago she was still living.
I could see her standing there
Listening to you and your son.

The sword is drawn at last. She
Has impaled herself on it.

*Theseus crosses the stage. He lifts her face, brushes
the hair from her forehead, looks silently into her
dead eyes, finally lets her head fall with a sigh.*

THESEUS
  She dropped the cup, but there's no wine spilled.
  She must have drunk it all. That's a lot
  Of wine for a young woman to drink,
  Her father was a big-headed man.
  She must have been drunk. I guess she was
  Out of her senses when she did it.

*The Second Chorus bring in Hippolytus, dead, his
arms and legs obviously broken, smeared with dirt
and blood.*

THESEUS
  What has happened? Is he badly hurt?

II CHORUS
  When he went to get his horse
  The bull trampled him to death.
  We were too late to save him.
  One of the grooms was killed, too.
  The bull broke down the barn doors,
  And escaped in the darkness.

THESEUS
  Let them lie together on this couch.
  Just a little while ago, I guess
  They must have been happy lying here.
  What a terrible thing to happen.
  And so suddenly. I should have stayed
  Away. I am a good-natured man.

But everywhere I bring disaster.
I am just Theseus, a bawdy
Old campaigner, why should things like this
Have to happen to me all the time?

I Chorus

The sword of a Russian witch,
Proud past belief, the evil
Memory of a bestial
Queen long dead.

They could not win.
Her love was not strong enough,
And her vanity took flesh.

His frail pride could not withstand
That lewd hungry animal.
It walked forth alive from him.

Out of vision generate
The perfected grace of bliss,
The terrible things that wait
Behind substance, seeking form.

Impure intention is damned
By the act it embodies.

Each sinned with the other's virtue.

They go out of the darkness,
Onto a road of darkness.

The wind turns to the north, and
The leaves rattle. An unknown
Bird cries out. And the insects
Of a day die in the starlight.

IPHIGENIA AT AULIS

IPHIGENIA AT AULIS

First Chorus, two people
Second Chorus, four people

Agamemnon
Iphigenia
Achilles

The Greek Heroic Age
The seawall above the Bay of Aulis

At the back of the stage, a screen seven feet high and ten feet wide with two tones of grey, for sea and sky. Along the bottom of this screen is a step about one foot high. At the right and left are screens, seven feet high and four feet wide.

On the step, at right and left, sit the First Chorus. At the right is a young girl, dressed only in a short tight black wrapper, like a sarong, gaudily jewelled, highly painted, a street prostitute. At the left is a fat old man, with shaved head, wrapped in a white cloth, a small brass bowl beside him, a beggar. The First Chorus speak with great dignity and treat the principals with a certain condescension. All business with the principals is done by them.

*The Second Chorus sit, two and two, along the walls
on either side, in front of the screens. They are incon-
spicuously dressed, possibly in long blue gowns. They
are the musicians, mob, commentators, prop men and
sound effects.*

*Iphigenia is dressed like the prostitute, but without the
jewelry and makeup.*

*Achilles wears a white cloth, with his arms and chest
bare, tied with a cord around his waist, the way In-
dians are supposed to wear blankets, but somewhat
shorter. This is the same costume as the beggar's.*

*Agamemnon is dressed in a simplified version of a
light-armed Greek soldier's costume, with a short
sword and a fiddle-shaped shield. The sword is in a
plain scabbard, has a cruciform hilt, looks rather like
a child's wooden sword. Agamemnon wears heavy
boots, the rest are barefoot.*

*Iphigenia's red robe should completely envelop her.
Achilles' should give the appearance of a military cape.
Both are plain rectangles of very bright scarlet. Other-
wise, there are no colors except black and white.*

There are no other props.

*At the beginning the stage is dark; on the screen, reach-
ing from the painted horizon to the ground, is a path
of light, the moonpath on the sea. There is a similar*

*rectangle of light on the floor of the stage. The light
on the screen is thrown from behind, that on the floor
from directly overhead. Towards the end of the play,
day breaks and the stage grows rapidly lighter; the
last lights should come up suddenly, with an effect of
dazzling brightness. The dances should be restrained,
formal, very slow. They should largely be confined to
the space defined by the path of light on the floor.*

*The make-up should be as formal as possible, or, much
better, the principals and the First Chorus should wear
masks and rope wigs, except for the beggar, who is
completely bald.*

I Chorus
　No wind has blown for a month.

　Under the moon the water
　Is as still as ice, the light
　Like a pavement on the sea,
　Like snow.

　The ships lie like stones.

　Nothing moves in the stillness
　But the stars in the rigid
　Heaven.

　The ships are frozen
　In the warm midsummer sea.
　The worms eat them and they rot.

The souls of men rot, frozen
In the sea of illusion.

II Chorus

This bay is a good harbor.
It doesn't freeze in winter.

There's something out there, moving,
Black in the moonlit water.

I see two black spots, like seals.

Those aren't seals. Those are people.

I can hear them call over
The surf; it is so quiet.

It is Iphigenia
And the young king, Achilles.

It's her. I can hear her laugh.

They play together like fish.

When they dive through the water,
Their bodies are black, and then
Flash in the moonlight, like fish.

One of them has disappeared.
There's only one black spot now.

They're swimming in each other's
Arms with their heads together.

They are coming ashore now.

How beautiful she is. Look.

Speak lower. They will hear you.

I Chorus

Her wet thighs are all on fire.
They break the surf as proud as
Salmon move up waterfalls.

A halo envelops her.
Her shoulders prance in the spray,
Like young goats in the mountains.

Her legs are around his waist;
And their lips are together.

They stand at the water's edge,
Swaying, knotted together,
Like the sea tangle that sways,
Back and forth in the sea's wash,
In the place where the whales play.

He is lying on the sand.
She is standing over him,
Shaking water from her hair.
The drops sparkle like fireflies.

She is dancing over him,
Whirling a whip of seaweed.

They have awakened the sea birds.
They fly around them crying,
Confused in the moonlight.

II Chorus

Hark.
I heard the ring of metal
On stone. Someone is coming
Along the seawall.

It is
Agamemnon, the old king.

He has his old dog with him.

Watch him. Look how he stumbles.

Is he walking in his sleep?

Sleepwalkers never stumble.

He certainly acts confused.

Maybe he has been drinking.

He is an awful drunkard.

Agamemnon enters.

AGAMEMNON
What is that ring of stars on the skyline?
How bright they are. It is nearly morning.

I CHORUS
The Necklace of Artemis.
It is midsummer midnight.

AGAMEMNON
I don't notice the stars much; but I think
One of them is brighter than usual.

I CHORUS
It is. When the heavens swing
Full circle, the Beardriver,
At midsummer, at midnight,
Crosses from darkness to light.

The Hunting Dogs drive the Bears
In a narrowing circle.
The axis of the world grinds
On the Dragon's writhing tail.
The Lion vomits the Sun.
The Yeoman of Artemis
Hands her necklace from the Moon
To the Sun; and a jewel
Bursts into flames.

It is said
In each jewel in that necklace
You can see every other
Jewel reflected and itself
Reflected in every one.

AGAMEMNON
I don't understand. It sounds ominous.

I CHORUS
There are always things like that
Happening in the heavens.

AGAMEMNON
How still it is. Even the birds are still.
Usually you can't hear them for the waves.
Now the surf is only a faint murmur.
It is a byword to speak of the wind
As dying. I think, this time, it is dead.

I CHORUS
Can't you sleep?

AGAMEMNON

No. The glare of the moonlight
Outside my tent wakes me. And the quiet
Keeps me awake. I thought I heard the birds
Cry, and voices.

I CHORUS

You did. The princess
And Achilles are down there
On the beach. They were swimming
In the moonlight.

AGAMEMNON

How she loves to swim.
She'd spend all her time swimming and hunting
If she could. We used to swim together
When she was little, just a few years ago.
Now she has a lover to swim with her.
A girl turns to a woman overnight.
When she was born he was a puppy;
And they played together on a bearskin.
It was wonderful—two young animals.
Now he's such an old dog, he's almost blind.
Look, Rex, look at the moon. He doesn't know
It's there. He smells my finger and whimpers.
He can't understand a pointing finger.
I don't suppose men are any wiser.
I don't know one who can tell ends from means.
Here we are, all Greece, crazy for a war
That's none of our business. A lot of us
Will die chasing a cuckold's fancy wife.
Maybe none of us will ever get home.

If we do, it won't be the same again.
What if I gave the order to turn back?
I wonder. Maybe the wind would blow then.
We're going to pay a terrible price
To get out of here otherwise. I know.
I don't need any wars, I've had enough.
I can imagine much better battles
Than were ever fought. Do you know that I
Have lain in bed whole nights, and watched armies
March and countermarch around my big toe?
I'm sure as much good came of those battles
As any real ones I've ever fought in.

I CHORUS

At any rate, less evil;
And what was gained was soon lost.

The conjunctions of the world
Are unstable by nature.

It is a foolhardy thing
To throw the torch of action
In the straw of consequence.

AGAMEMNON

That's true. But it's a world of consequence.
We are bound by the power of dead acts.
And that power grows and grows, more and more,
Until no man can see the end of it.
Some day it will break down of its own weight.
You live as best you can, though you can see
No meaning in responsibility.
You choose the greater or the lesser good.

Warriors, politicians, and most kings are
Kind to their families. Saints and saviors
Deny their mothers and dare not marry.
Once you've started, you can never turn back.

I Chorus

In the turmoil of the waves
Of the world, let the heart learn
From the gull that sleeps alone
In the midst of the ocean.

Agamemnon

Those soldiers have that sort of innocence.
What do they care about the agony
Of responsibility? You assume
The liability of the world's sin,
The sin I make as a man of affairs.
They assume nothing but the summer night.
The poor enjoy moonlight and perfumed air
In strict proportion to their poverty,
Whether it is voluntary or not.

I Chorus

You're wrong. But I won't argue.

Agamemnon goes out.

II Chorus

Look at that old hypocrite.
Everybody knows he's been
His own daughter's lover since
The day she was big enough
To take him. She's plenty bold

68

Enough about it. It's no
Secret. Now he's marrying
Her off for "reasons of state."

The rich and powerful do
Whatever suits their fancy.
They'd hang one of us if they
Caught us doing the same things.

They say he's in love with one
Of Achilles' concubines.

I think he sees Achilles
Becoming too strong for him
In this war, unless he has
Someone there to keep him down.

O, she'll keep him down all right.
She'll be the one'll give orders.
He'll be lucky if she leaves
Him strength to carry them out.

If she wanted to weaken me,
I wouldn't mind it a bit.

Iphigenia and Achilles enter.

ACHILLES
Do I love your body's beauty,
Its fair harmony of movement,
The fire of your eyes, and the sweet
Melody of your varying voice?
Do I love the different perfumes
Of your breasts and armpits and thighs,
And the honey of your mouth and sex,

And your limbs that clasp me about?
I love more your secret splendor,
Melody, fragrance, and sweetness,
And your secret, hidden embrace.
Space cannot contain that shining,
Time bear away that melody,
That sweetness ever be consumed,
No weariness ever sunder
The embrace in which we two cling.

IPHIGENIA

I have only love, nothing else.
I feel as though there were nothing
Else in me but you. I have no
Being but what fills me with you,
Like a mirror filled with the sun.
I see world upon world in me,
Like diamonds in that sunlight.

ACHILLES

Love is a terrifying thing.
I can feel it spread out from us
In a flood deep as this moonlight,
Drowning the mountains of the world.

IPHIGENIA

The fish do not drown in the sea,
Nor the birds fall that tread the air.
Gold does not turn black in the fire.
It does not rust away with time.
The burning years and wasting fire
Only make it shine more brightly.

Everything lives by its nature.
I live in you and in your love,
As pure spirits live in vision.

ACHILLES

One should trust the power of love
When one feels it inside oneself.
Still, it's a frightening thing to have.

IPHIGENIA

I can see now that what I thought
Was myself was just a desert
Before you came to me; and what
I thought were plants were only stones.
You plowed me with your sharp manhood,
Rained on me with your sweet manhood,
Shone on me with your hot manhood,
And comforted me in the night
With the dew of your tenderness;
And all the pain of my shut heart
Has broken out into thousands
And thousands of flowers. O love,
Take me, hold me in the drenching
Moonlight. Hold me. I am perishing.

ACHILLES

We can never perish. It is
Unlove and unhate that give form
To phantasms of time and space.
See how the moonlight falls out of
The immense sky, as pure as love,
And freezes the waves of the sea.

71

Remember, all the waves of all
The oceans that have come ashore
On all the beaches of the world
Since time began, and ever shall,
Have a number; and there shall come
A time that number shall be totalled.
And so these doomed few feet of flesh,
Mingled together in one fire,
Each self knowing in the other,
Hold, and hold back, and sum up, all
The world's origin and decay.

IPHIGENIA

Think. This is the last night. This is
All. O love. I cannot bear it.
This war will last for years, and I
Will have nothing to keep me warm
In the cold north but these hours
Falling away through the long nights.
No one but yellow savages,
Clothed in the mangled skins of beasts.
Hold me back. Fill me with yourself.
Leave me with yourself inside me,
Our compound flesh a walking
Memory. Let the uncanny
Calm of our lust's vision take form.
Lover. There is only tonight.
O sweet lover. I wish I were
Prolific as fish in the sea,
Or the teeming flies of the air.
The glory that doubles itself
In us can manifest itself

72

Only in what streams between us,
Wrung from the knot of love.

ACHILLES

So late.
There is so little time left us.
I have come to love you so late.
All the past and all the future
Are consumed in love more ancient
Than all the past, new beyond all
The future. I do not believe
That this present will ever pass;
That the sun which steals upon us,
Beneath our feet, can steal us from
Each other.
Don't go. Stay with me.
Let Troy keep that pink bitch in heat.
Let other vagrants seduce her.
Her life will end, covered with scabs,
A bawd amongst barbarians.
Your foolish uncle will only
Lose her again if his betters
Buy her back for him with their blood.
A born whore and a born cuckold—
Why should good men die for them?

IPHIGENIA

No.
It's not circumstance that matters,
But the purity of the deed.
The affairs of men are always
Trivial, and the important

Is always sacrificed to them.
The goddess will release the winds
If I devote myself to her
For ten years as priestess in the North.
Only I can free the Greek ships.
I do not care if they sail out
And founder, and never reach Troy;
My part will be done. When I am
Ready, the sails of my ship will
Fill with wind. The fleet can follow
Me or not, just as they see fit.

II Chorus
The old king is coming back.

Iphigenia
I want to talk to my father
Alone. I may never see him
Again. I'll come back to you soon.
We'll be together till daybreak.

Achilles
Hurry. We have so little time.

Iphigenia
I won't be long. Kiss me once more.

Achilles goes out.

Iphigenia
He is innocent as a child.

I CHORUS

The beauty of the warrior
Is the wisdom of the child.

IPHIGENIA

Am I beautiful? Am I wise?

I CHORUS

You are very beautiful;
Beautiful with the other
Face of wisdom, the end of guile.
The world has been found and lost
In corruption since you were
As spotless as he is now.
The egg's unbroken oval
Is his mathematics, and yours
The graph of the skull's sutures.

IPHIGENIA

I am as capable as you
Of oblivious love, or you
Of sacrifice.

I CHORUS

Who doubts it?
We are only reflections
Of the warrior and the queen.

They are images of us.

Consequence dogs your father.
You know it is only
Possibility seen backwards.

You will act past consequence,
Choose past possibility,
Know past the meaning of truth,
As you have desired past act.

You know what you are doing.
Only the beautiful know.

That is a definition
Of beauty, perhaps the best.

IPHIGENIA

I am sacrificing myself
To myself, to unlock the vast
Waterwheel of blind history,
And let it turn in my heart's blood.
And I do it without effort,
Or very little. If it cost
Me nothing, I would be a myth,
Not a woman.

Iphigenia goes out.

I CHORUS

The sands have
Run out in the hour glass.
It is the moment before
The absorbed reader starts from
His book and turns the egg full
Of dust to the top.

II CHORUS

Wake up.
Here he comes again, snooping.

76

I wish he'd get a hot boy
To keep him warm in bed. Then
Maybe he'd keep his old nose
Out of other folk's business.

If I had on my conscience
All the stuff he has on his,
I don't think I'd ever sleep.

Watch her now, how she'll snuggle
Up to him. They'll put their heads
Together and hatch some scheme
To swindle poor Achilles.

He's got a head of his own.
He'll get the better of them yet.
He's a great man, Achilles.
All his soldiers worship him.
He eats just the same rations
As they do.

The Myrmidons
Are all equals. He's only
The leader. Nobody is
Better than anybody
Else with them. That's why they're called
Myrmidons. They're like the ants.
Each man does his proper job,
And draws from the common fund.

Ants have queens.

But they don't rule.
They perpetuate the race.

She's pretty crazy about
Achilles. I wonder what
The old man would do if he
Thought she would ever tell him
She'd been her father's mistress.

He'd probably murder her.

Achilles is too good a man
For that old fox and his pup.

Iphigenia and Agamemnon enter.

AGAMEMNON
   You should have told him. He's bound to find out.

IPHIGENIA
   It will be too late then. But how
   Will he discover it? No one
   Will know but you and my own maid.
   The fleet will sail and him with it.
   The war will be over before
   He learns I was not on the ship
   Which first turned to the wind. Besides,
   He'll not see the end of this war.
   Beauty like his dies violently.
   His body will be dragged in dust,
   Black with blood, and battle-trampled,
   Till it has turned to potter's clay.

AGAMEMNON
   Is that surmise or prophecy?

IPHIGENIA

Neither.
It is fact. I know Fate's logic
And the selling price of Fortune.

AGAMEMNON

It may be. The whole thing terrifies me.
Why do you have to involve me in it?
What if you're wrong? Suppose nothing happens?

IPHIGENIA

I am not wrong. It will happen.
I can trust you to be silent.
I can trust your love for me.

AGAMEMNON

Why not use Achilles? He loves you more.

IPHIGENIA

Loves me enough to cut my throat?
Hasn't life taught you anything?

AGAMEMNON

I know. I know. I want no part of it.
It's three months ago, the first day of spring,
The wind died as we reefed sail in this place.
You came to me that night and told me why,
And what must be done. I haven't slept since.
Everyone thinks I have dysentery.
For three months I have been dying of dread.
Now my courage is all gone. I'm afraid
Of everything, of you, of Achilles,

Of my own guards. Even my old dog scares me
When he growls and quivers and dreams of bears.
Do you know what frightens me most of all?
The indifferent gaze of that beggar
And whore who sit together day and night,
There on the seawall. I can't keep away
From them. I spend hours talking to them.
I'm afraid of their passionless faces.
It's not worth it. We can burn the ships
And march overland, conquering the country
As we go. This is the greatest army
In the world. We can make it an empire.
They would follow Achilles anywhere.
Why waste the youth of Greece to ruin Troy?
You could be a queen of queens, mightier
Than Minos or the Egyptian Pharaohs.
I would rather we turn back. You're worth more
Than Helen, more than any victory.

IPHIGENIA

I have been the Queen of Heaven
And Earth, the Living Artemis.
The Moon will turn full at sunrise.
In her name I shall wed the Sun,
And vanish in their doubled light.

AGAMEMNON

That's fine for you. I'm left with guilty hands.

IPHIGENIA

You are that expedient thing—
A king of the world. Can you be

More or less guilty than you are?
Let my blood be on my own head.
Besides, this is nothing but talk.
Try it. Order them to turn back.
You know no one would obey you.
You are only the first amongst
Equals. Suppose you persuaded
The other kings, you know the ranks
Would revolt and find new leaders.
As soon turn back a falling stone
As wake the awful sloth of war.
Of course I'm worth more than victory;
Any life is, more than any
Victory. The poorest sentient
Life is worth more than all the states
That ever fought or ever will.
What does that prove? I die by my
Own values. And the ships sail out
In the wind of my deed to ends
That have as little to do with
Good and evil as the dust motes
My breath disturbs in the sunlight.
They'd say it was expedient
That one die for the good of all.
If you want it made public, ask them.
You'll soon find out. Ask that soldier.

AGAMEMNON

I know. Certainly, I know what he'd say.
But you've no right to treat me as a means
To your salvation. I've myself to save.

The power of Artemis lives in you.
You can command the wind if you want to.

IPHIGENIA

The maneuvers of the navy,
Like the conquest of a city,
Are the concerns of the power
Of a king, not mine, nor the god's.
Make my ends yours. You'll not be used.

AGAMEMNON

Can I undo a lifetime's means and ends
Between now and daybreak? I inhabit
Another universe. It was too late for that
Before I was born. Perhaps she'll consent
If we go through the acts of ritual.
The appearances would be satisfied.
She could snatch you out from under the knife
At the last moment. She has done such things
Before. She would do anything for you.

IPHIGENIA

The hawk dies rather than eat grain.
There is a moral universe
In which the whole contains the parts,
And each part contains the whole.
Do you want me to ask someone
Else?

AGAMEMNON

No.

IPHIGENIA

Then be quiet. Hold me
In your arms and kiss me. I am
A child you are always leaving
To go to war. Always kissing
Goodbye, with your sword in your hand.

AGAMEMNON

I can think of nothing worth such a price.

IPHIGENIA

Be still. You bought and paid for me
When you begot me. I am all
The girls your soldiers have butchered
In all the wars you've ever fought;
All the slattern camp followers
Who have given them the comforts
Of filthy bodies and rank wine,
And sealed their loves with sores and lice.
I am the babies they fathered
In haste, and died, and never saw.
Artemis—the Net of the Fish
Of Heaven—I am the fleshy
Net in which you have caught the world.
Twenty years ago black serpents
Writhed in the Sun, and I came out
Of you a spasm of ecstasy.
When the Moon's disc slides into full,
And her face becomes featureless
As a pure mirror, I return.
We live here tonight with my head
In your lap, my hands in your beard;

83

We are the oldest kind of lovers.
There are two eggs in me must hatch
As apparitions in the sky—
Twin children of the beginning
And end of the wisdom of war.

They dance. The dance comes slowly and power-
fully to climax. Agamemnon steps into the dark-
ness and Achilles takes his place. The dance is re-
solved and Iphigenia and Achilles come forward.

IPHIGENIA

In your body lies all my joy.
My heart is breaking like a shell.
I feel my courage drain from me.
I will be alone and never
Hear your voice in the long winter,
As I sit and think of your ways.
I will never see the young hawk
Wheel in heaven, nor the wolfhound
And the stag running together,
But the memory of your grace
Will come upon me and stun me.
The days will be long without you,
As they vanished like the closing
Of an eye when I was with you.
I was never weary with you,
Achilles. I shall be weary
Without you. My eyes will go blind
Staring after your memory.

ACHILLES

I shall come to you when the war

Is over, when Troy has fallen.
And the world is quiet again.
I shall sail northward, seeking you,
When Helen returns to the Greeks.
Love betrayed has brought this trouble
On the world; and the faith we keep
Will last beyond all the ruin
Of that sly, rose-garlanded woman.
A love beyond time can suffer
No parting. Those who love beyond
The world, space cannot separate.

Very slowly they begin to dance.

ACHILLES

When I lie in your arms it seems
A cloud of fire comes over us,
And lightning shines along the ground;
The earth moves as I enter you,
And the corpuscles of our blood
Change to coruscations of light;
As I look in your entranced eyes,
I see mirrored there a glory
Beyond the illusion of the world.
I merge with its mirrored image,
And pass from glory to glory.

IPHIGENIA

Every part of me that is not
Lost in you has melted away.
All my senses are lost in you.
I have no speech to speak of you.

I am drowned in you like the sea.
Nothing is within me but you.
Nothing is without me but you.
I have fallen into the Sun,
Into the starless heart of dark.

*Their dance gives an impression of terrific violence
under tremendous restraint. Though they exhaust
themselves in climax after climax, the dance never be-
comes rapid, but remains extremely slow. The stage
is darkened, then grows light again. They lie quietly
on the steps while the Chorus speak, and then come
forward.*

I CHORUS

She has conceived twice tonight.

Nourished beyond time, her womb
Grows in the crystal heaven,
And in the earth's iron heart,
And opens in time's fulness.

Molten rock boils from the earth.
Comets wander in heaven.

The shifting balance quivers
To a stop; and her twin sons
Walk abroad on earth and sky.

One wears jewels in his hair.
He is clothed in golden gauze.
Dragons bear up his swift feet.
Burning coals are in his hands.

One is clothed in webs of stars.
And the Pole stars crown his head.
Glowing planets shoe his feet.
Cataclysms glove his hands.

The diamond of compassion
And wisdom grows forever
In the bowels of the earth.

Unmoving and unmoved, the star
Of benevolence and light
Shines in heaven's still center.

II Chorus

A cloud passed over the moon.

Did it? I was asleep.

Look.
There it is, off to the west.
A little, floating, white cloud.

I was falling asleep, too,
But the shadow woke me up.

I wonder if it means wind.

It means something. It didn't
Climb in the sky by itself.

Iphigenia

That is all. Leave me quickly now.
The sky pales. It is almost day.
Go to your ship. Make sure they are
Ready. You must be first to sail

After me. Embrace me once more.
Tell me you love me and then go.
When the Sun stands on the Earth's lips
A wind from the Moon will hurl me
To my responsibility.
You must be quick. It will not blow
Forever. It will be a long
Time before this chance comes again.
Lover. It is for the glory
We have created together
That I act. There is no other
Way it can be made manifest.
You must obey without question.

ACHILLES

I act only as your creature.
I have given you my will. You
Have taken my understanding.
Hereafter, I move in the world
As our memory incarnate,
Like one who walks a rope of dreams.

IPHIGENIA

O sweet, sweet Achilles, only
Our shadows will meet again, thrown
On the fragile screen of sleep.

ACHILLES

Night after night, to start awake,
Grope in the dark, and find nothing.

IPHIGENIA

O lover. Stop. It is not right.

We are letting the dream destroy
Reality. We sleep in dark
Apart, wake in light together.
Never forget that. On the plain
Of Troy, in the squalor of war,
Never forget, the ruinous
Face of Helen is illusion.
I conquer Helen forever.
When you dream in a cloud of battle,
Open your eyes on my face.
Talk no more. We have said enough.
I have made two red robes for us
To meet this morning's sunrise in.
I will dress you in yours and you
Help me with mine.

ACHILLES

You are weeping.

IPHIGENIA

Yes. The dawn flickers in the sky,
As we help each other to dress,
As we have so many mornings.
Dear, I am only a young girl.
Now I am clothed in your heart. You
Are clothed in mine. We cannot part.
Stand there and let me look at you.
I kiss you goodbye. Go now. Go.

Achilles goes out.

IPHIGENIA

Stand forth. Prepare me for pure act.

Wash me. My lips and thighs and breasts.
I go to a blazing bride bed.

I Chorus

Your breasts are two doves. Your eyes
Are doves' eyes. Between your thighs
Is a nest of nightingales.

Iphigenia

Anoint me. Put perfume and oil
On all my passages of sense,
On hands and feet that did my will,
On the sex with which I loved.

I Chorus

Your sandaled feet are lovely.
Love is quick in your hands. Love
Swoons in the wine of your sex.

Iphigenia

Bind my feet with tangled flowers,
The summer flowers of the Sun.
Weave flowers in my hair, the white
Moon flowers that waste in the dawn.

I Chorus

Feet that glided like swallows,
Hair that shimmered like moonlight,
You burn like the morning star.

Iphigenia

Draw my red robe close about me.

Seal me away in my own fire.
Crown me with laurel and flowers
Of marjoram. I conquer Troy.
I marry the burning daylight.

My father waits at the headland.
The sea turns white before sunrise.

She goes out.

I CHORUS
She stands before her father.

The first gold ray of the sun
Shines on the knife.

Her robe falls.

She is enveloped in fire.

Her beauty is terrible,
More beautiful than ranked ships,
And drawn swords, than the forest
Of spears, than the long banners
That lift as the wind begins.

The knife is black with her blood.

Heaven has taken her. She
Has gone into the bright world.

The flames crawl over Troy's walls.
Asia falls into ruin.
Aeneas and Odysseus
Wander, lost in a new world.
Helen dies in a brothel.

BEYOND THE MOUNTAINS

I—HERMAIOS

HERMAIOS

The action takes place from twilight to midnight on the eve of the first night of the Christian era, on a terrace before the summer palace in the hills above the Bactrian Greek city of Alexandria-in-the-Paropamisadae, overlooking a cliff, from which the city itself is supposed to be visible below in the distance. In modern terms, this is the foothills of the Hindu Kush, in Afghanistan.

First Chorus, a beggar and prostitute.
Second Chorus, four or six persons.

Hermaios Soter.
Kalliope, his wife and sister.
Demetrios, his brother.
Tarakaia, his mistress.
Berenike, his daughter.
Menander, his son.

Against the back wall is a long panel, painted with a black and white sketch of a high snow mountain, shaped rather like the Matterhorn. In front of it is a screen, seven feet high and ten feet wide, with leaves opening like a double door in the middle. Along the bottom of this screen is a step, one foot high. The leaves of the screen stand slightly open until the last exit of Hermaios and Tarakaia, when they are shut for a few moments. The land is imagined to fall away to the back and left. Entrances and exits are made as in the Roman stage, "from the country" at the left front, "from the town and house" at the right.

On the step, at right and left, sit the First Chorus. At the right is a young girl, dressed only in a tight, black, very short, sarong-like wrapper, gaudily jeweled, highly painted—a street prostitute. At the left is a fat old man, with shaved head, wrapped in a white cloth, secured with a rope around his waist and draped over his shoulders, leaving his chest bare, the way Indians are supposed to wear blankets, but somewhat shorter. At his side is a small brass bowl—he is a beggar. Both are barefoot, and masked. The girl wears a black wig. They speak with great dignity and treat the principals with a certain condescension. Unless otherwise mentioned, all business with the principals is done by them.

The Second Chorus sit, two by two, along the wall on either side, towards the front. They are inconspicuously dressed, possibly in long dull blue gowns, the same for both sexes, and wear soft-soled shoes. They are the musicians, mob, commentators, prop men and sound effects. Their instruments should include flute or recorders, horn or musette, violin or viola, zither or similar instrument, and percussion, which should include small drums, small cymbals, triangle, and resonant wood. At the lines "Without warning their horns roared," a contra bass brass, bass fiddle, contra bassoon, one or all, can sound their lowest notes, off stage.

Hermaios is dressed exactly like the beggar, and is barefoot. His mask should be canny, with a small black beard and thin hair.

Kalliope wears a very sheer white sari, white sandals, and a diadem, a plain gold ribbon. Her mask should be haughty and pale blonde.

Tarakaia is dressed, on her first entrance, like the prostitute, but with better taste in jewelry. On her second entrance, she wears a black cloth like the white one of Hermaios. Where it falls away in motion her body is nude and very white. She wears a red rope wig. Her mask should be extremely intense with abnormally large and protruding eyes.

Berenike is dressed like Tarakaia, but without jewelry. Her mask should be a younger edition of Tarakaia's with a less dérangée and stricken look.

Demetrios wears a simplified version of a light-armed Greek soldier's costume, with pleated kilt, black sandals, and a short sword in a black and white scabbard. It should be obvious that this warlike costume is purely ornamental. His mask is an innocent, slightly spoiled face, a red beard and curly hair.

The dancers who take the part of Huns should be

dressed in brilliant colors, high buskins, lots of gold embroidery, massive eyebrows, very long moustaches, but no beards—black, red, and blue face paint, two long pheasants' feathers in each headdress.

The cloak for Hermaios is a very bright crimson six-foot square of heavy material. All the weapons used in the battle dance should be as spectacular as possible—trident, halberd, double swords, plumed spears. The āxe in Tarakaia's last dance should be small and simple. Hermaios and Tarakaia may enter as if riding imaginary horses. There are no other properties, except the beggar's bowl, Hermaios' diadem, Tarakaia's noose, and a large rhinestone, with which light should be flashed in the audience's eyes as Tarakaia gives the ring to the Second Chorus.

At the opening the general lighting is slightly dim, and grows rapidly darker, to more than medium dimness, for the rest of the play. At the same time, a square of light comes up, illuminating the screen and the floor in front of it from the upper left. There can be a faintly bluish light, behind the screen, shining on the mountain, but it should be used with restraint.

Except for the crimson robe, the beggar's bowl, and the jewelry, the colors should be exclusively black and white, excepting of course the Huns, who should be as gaudy as possible.

The metal percussion should only be used in the battle

*dance, the musette or horn only there and in a flourish
before the first entrance of Hermaios and Tarakaia.*

For the historical background, see W. W. Tarn, The
Greeks in Bactria and India, *and the* Cambridge An-
cient History *and* History of India. *Coins of Hermaios
can be seen in large museum collections. I am aware
that the conquerors of Bactria were of unknown Cen-
tral Asian origin, and probably not Huns.*

I Chorus
   The twilight has gone like breath.

   In the sharp starlight the snow
   Stretches endlessly away
   Into the dark at the foot
   Of the mountains, like the white sands
   On all the beaches of the sea.

   The wind comes and goes with a sound
   Like a vast concourse of people.

II Chorus
   Demetrios and the queen
   Have been amusing themselves,
   Fishing through the forming ice.

I Chorus
   The salmon as it plunges
   Upward in the waterfall

Cannot see or touch itself,
And so it can never know
What sort of creature it is.

Only the weight of the abyss
Can force the eel's unwilling birth.

II Chorus

Midwinter night. Off to the east
The star burns brighter than ever.

It's so bright it casts a shadow.

One by one the planets have moved
Into place around it. Tonight
All the wheels have meshed. The whirling
Equinoxes have closed their term.

Their figures were correct. Somewhere
Tonight it will meet the midnight
At the zenith.

Thirty degrees
Or more to the west, near the sea—
Somewhere in the cold Syrian
Desert, under the desert stars.

The goddesses that loved the Greeks
Sprang forth from the thundering sky,
Or rose, wet with love, from the sea.
The desert will give up this god,
A baby of blood in the dark,
A burning baby from the ice.

I Chorus

The razor edge of starlight cuts
The sweet white womb of the aloe.

The lily of a century
Is a thousand-branched candlestick.

The lily of a myriad years
Is a baby whose extended
Arms branch into infinity.

II Chorus

Hermaios should have gone along.

He's a strange man. He agreed
With them. I think he was sure
They were right. In fact, I think
He was more sure than they, yet
He did nothing about it.

That's a long way to go. Gods
Are born in the neighborhood
Every year.

What's distance to him?
He's run over half the world,
Putting the face of empire
On howling chaos, patching
Up a rotting make believe
That's tumbling around his ears
Tonight.

It won't be tonight.

No, he'll pull us through again,
Just like he's done it before.

I should think he'd get out, while
The getting's good. This may be
The last chance he'll ever have.

He fought three wars in India,
And marched to the gates of China.
He can go where he's a mind to.

It's a cold winter. A trip
Like that costs a lot of money.
Nothing might come of it.
The Romans might kidnap him.

You talk a lot of nonsense.
I suppose he just couldn't
Stand the expense? He hasn't
Got anything but money left.

We buy the suburbs each year
From a new enemy.

We've done it for ten years now.
We may last another ten.

He's down there tonight, buying
Another year for the last
Of Alexander's cities,
From this year's gang of brigands.

Hermaios is not a free man.
All the acts of all the Greeks
Hold him in place with the soft clench

Of all their busy centuries.
He'd have gone if he had to crawl,
But his star moves the other way,
And its light goes down by itself.
Do you realize that the Greeks
Are almost gone? As the prophet
Foretold, Troy has won in the end.
Rome and the barbarian rule
Or ruin all but one last town,
So remote it is forgotten.
Peddlers, gamblers, whoremasters,
Roman slaves, Buddhist monks, craftsmen
And courtesans for Chinamen
And Negroes, at the opposite
End of the earth. Oh, we've gone far,
And this is all that's left of Greece,
One city in a wilderness
Herodotus peopled with monsters.

Gaspar, Melchior, Balthasser,
They're not Greeks, but the old Asia,
So corrupt with blood they live on
Cabbage and can't even kill lice.
They went back, putting toe to heel
In Alexander's iron footprints.
Now it will all be done over.
Someday this winter journey west
Will be a ritual procession
In this new god's religion.
Hermaios holds the doom of the Greeks
Alive in him in the shadow
Of the peaks at the earth's navel.

It looks to me like he'd get doom,
A bellyfull of it. The queen
Is restless in her dirty bed.

Do you think he knows what goes on?

I don't see how he could miss it.

He's been away most of the time.

I don't like this brother-sister
Business. It has brought ruin
To all the kings of the Greek world.

Just like animals, any flaw
In a family is bred in
Until it destroys it.

Evil
Grows as the rose petals double.

The wife of one brother, the whore
Of the other. She must have been
A lovely child.

As a matter
Of fact, she was. I remember.
But she's been deranged ever since
She lost her first child in India.
She was captured and sacrificed
In one of their bloody temples.

The queen always blamed Hermaios.

Since he has taken that Indian witch
For a mistress, I think she's come
To believe he did it himself.

Demetrios feeds her with hate.
He's always envied his brother.

They caught something from that redhead.
They've all been different since she came.

Have you noticed that the princess
Looks like her daughter, not the queen's?

She's infected the whole family.
Menander is in love with her.

I guess she makes the king happy.

I wouldn't want any of her.

I couldn't get much sleep with her
Throwing fits in bed.

It's the queen
That terrifies me. She's so cold
And lewd and white, with her long neck
And white face like a vindictive
Swan.

Spit. You shouldn't have said that.

Why not?

It's a bad omen.

Omen or not, I don't know what
You're talking about, and I don't
Think you do either. Whenever
She comes towards me I remember
A hissing swan that terrified
Me when I was a little child.

You know, I've thought for a long time
That the queen was cooking something.
She's grown haughtier and much more
Self confident all this winter.

She certainly has got nothing
To be regal about. We're all
In the same sinking boat together.

And Demetrios makes himself
As scarce as possible.

May be.
If they are planning anything,
The blow will have to fall soon now.
Menander and Berenike,
Will be back before the new year.

Demetrios enters.

DEMETRIOS
The king and his girl are coming
From the city early tonight.
Let me know, the moment they come.

*He tosses a coin to one of the Second Chorus and
goes out. One of the Second Chorus reads the legend
on the coin.*

II CHORUS
Hermaios and Kalliope,
The Savior Gods. Saviors of what?
For what? They'd better get busy.
Menander and Berenike

The Guardian Gods. There's something
In Chinese. It's a coin minted
For the silk trade, and it looks like
It might serve as a gold spindle
To make a cord for a silk noose.
A privilege of crowned heads, I think.

Kalliope enters.

KALLIOPE

Has the king come back?

II CHORUS

No, lady,
He hasn't. And it will be late
When he does, if he does at all.
They may decide the time has come
To make beef of a dry cow.

KALLIOPE

No.
They've sense enough to understand
They can only sack the city
Once. There's too little left of us.
They've no seed to sow the desert
They'd make with their destruction.
But they can crop us every year.
A poor crop, but better than none.
And besides, they're afraid of her.
They look on her as the living
Artemis, the incarnation
Of the moon on earth. I suppose

107

It's that has held the king to her,
Really, all these years. She's no more
The same sex-crazy little girl
He picked up those long years ago.
The last few years have told on her.
It's a poor thing to have to change
From the goddess of a king's bed,
To a political convenience.

II CHORUS

I only hope they hurry up.
A summer capital is nice
To sit out a siege in, in summer.
We'll all freeze to death if they
Make a habit of winter warfare.

KALLIOPE

I am tired of the long cold, too.
And this thin air burns my nostrils,
Parches my skin and dries my hair.
There's never enough to breathe here.
The air is too thin to sing with,
And poor stuff for the gulp of love.
Even the stars burn without oil,
Like burning icicles. Twenty
Years ago we spent the winter
In the Vale of Kashmir. The stars
Were fat there, like the butter lamps
They burn in the temples. Something
Happened there. I've forgotten what.
Anyway, we never went back.
I guess we'll never go again.

Did you ever see the long white
Tentacles of the sun? I did,
Here, one winter. Later I dreamed
One of them reached out from the sky
Over the snow and curled into
My womb.

II CHORUS

Did it impregnate you?

KALLIOPE

No, it sucked everything out of me.

I CHORUS

The stars eat us as we eat dark.

KALLIOPE

The night is so black and the stars
Are terrible in the mountains.
No one would ever doubt they chart
Our doom, who saw them, cruel and pure,
Malignant over the last peaks.
I dream of them. Frightening dreams.

I CHORUS

The weaving circles of heaven
Are the orderly reflection
Of the erratic course of men
In eternity's still mirror.

Dreams are a drum music in code.
The world's great pulse in the small heart.

A subtle range of sound, seldom
Overheard except in sleep.

The troubled memories of pain
Seep thru the brain in sleep.
Men learn against their will.

Kalliope puts out her hand.

KALLIOPE

Snow. The wind is blowing the snow.
It's not living like fallen snow.
It's fine and dry like marble dust.
Soon it will drift over the roofs,
And seal us in for the winter.
I suppose it has a secret
Music, too. It has a sterile
Sort of geometry. I know
The one thin tune of its silence.
I don't find it interesting.

She goes out.

II CHORUS

Look! Look! Something is happening
Down in the city. They have lit
A beacon fire.

They crowd to the left rear of the stage.

There's another.

Two fires. That must be a signal.

They're celebrating peace down there.

The Huns have gone.

The siege is lifted.

Thank God! Tomorrow we can start
Back to the city, where it's warm.

There's another fire. A small one.
See it? Away from the others.

It must be in the suburbs.

The First Chorus come forward.

There are five—no—seven fires now.

They are hard to count.

They look like
A red Pleiades in the haze.

I Chorus
Those are not signal fires.

I know.
Go. Tell the queen the king has failed.
Alexandria-Beyond-the-Mountains
Is burning to the ground.

*One of the Second Chorus goes out. The First Chorus
return to their places.*

II Chorus
Who'd believe it? I always knew
It was bound to happen sometime.
I didn't think I'd live to see it.

Oh, no? After us the deluge?
The deluge doesn't always wait.

Time turns about. Troy wins at last.

Kalliope and Demetrios enter.

KALLIOPE

It's burning, all right. Such a small
Coal of fire in the distance like
A burnt out lamp wick. And that's all.
That little glowing spot burns up
All our past lives. Maybe that fire
Will light up some kind of future.
I feel as though I'd been sinking
In darkness for more years than I
Can remember.

DEMETRIOS

We have escaped.
That is a torch that will light us
Out of this labyrinth and back
To the Greek sea and Greek faces,
And humane ways. Now we can love
One another without intrigue,
Now we don't have to be afraid
Or ashamed anymore. At last
We are free. We can go away.
We can grow old together, in love,
In a better world. We are free
Of the hopelessness and bitterness
Of this place. We're not too old yet;
It happened in the nick of time.

If he isn't dead already
The king will die there and his girl
Along with him. All the money's here,
Except what he took for tribute;
And half the Greek troops are here.
In a year we will be walking
Under the olives, by the sea.
We will have forgotten this place,
The aimless struggle and the fear.

KALLIOPE

I wish I could believe that. No,
My dear, I'm afraid you're wrong. No.
Not tonight. Not ever. The only
Peace we're ever likely to enjoy
We had long ago when we lay
Wrapped in each other's arms in the womb.

DEMETRIOS

Don't talk that way. It isn't true.
We'll keep this day a holiday
For years to come. Beautiful years.

KALLIOPE

Those festivals will never be.
If what bound us together
Was as simple a thing as love,
May be our lives could drink its peace.
But it isn't, and what it is
Will keep the king alive awhile.
We three need each other. We are
Hungry ghosts that haunt each other.

Idle wishes won't call to life
A happy ending for three souls
Desire has locked in tragedy.

DEMETRIOS

We have suffered enough. I think
We have learned from that suffering
To want just to be let alone,
In peace, to love in our middle age.

KALLIOPE

A light has been born in darkness.
It may be our future glory,
But I doubt it. I think fate is
Burning our bridges ahead of us.

DEMETRIOS

Not fate but fortune. The balance
Of our lives swings up from hope
To happiness and freedom.

KALLIOPE

My dear.
If it were only true. We would
Be wiser, if we do not want
Our passions to destroy us, to act
As though we only had eight hours
To live. My darling. Take my hands
In yours. Tight. I am shuddering.
I am afraid of the eternal
Silence of these infinite spaces.
Oh, hide me, I am afraid, afraid.

I Chorus

The midwife's shears cut them apart.
They can never be joined again.

When they come together, nightmare
Struggles between them. A living
Gallows takes body from their kiss.

They have put their necks in the yoke
Of necessity. The winds of
Illusion whirl in their empty hearts.

Kalliope

How have we reached this time and place?
I was happy with Hermaios.
When I remember how happy,
I can hear something break in me.

Demetrios

I loved him too when we were young.
I thought he was the greatest man
In the world, when I was a boy.

Kalliope

My twin brother. Do I love you?
Have I anything to love with?
I think they cut it out of me,
And gave it to that madwoman,
There in India, long ago.
I am a statue moved by blood.

DEMETRIOS

 We have both been lost and heartless
 For years. Those years are over now.

KALLIOPE

 I am glad you think so. I have
 The horrible feeling everything
 Is slipping away from us.
 Soon that light will go out down there.
 There will be only pitch darkness
 To leap into. I feel as if
 I were about to be executed.

I CHORUS

 All the stars have gone out over
 The mountain.

 A storm is rising
 In the desert. It will break here
 Before morning.

II CHORUS

 There are lights down there on the road.
 They are moving.

 Those are torches.

 There are horsemen
 Coming up the road carrying
 Torches.

 I think it is the king.

 They are almost beneath us now.

I can see them. It's the king's guard,
But not the king or the priestess.

*A flourish. Hermaios and Tarakaia enter on horse-
back. One of the Second Chorus takes their horses.
The horses can be represented by riding whips, one
white, one black.*

I CHORUS

The king.

HERMAIOS

The king. Hermaios the Savior.
This is all he has left to save.

Kalliope runs up to him.

KALLIOPE

Oh! I am so glad you came back.
We saw the fires. I was frightened.

DEMETRIOS

We've all been worried. What happened?

HERMAIOS

Nothing we haven't been expecting
For years. It's all over now. Finished.
Let me rest awhile. I'm exhausted.
We fought for hours.

KALLIOPE

Are you wounded?

He looks at himself.

117

HERMAIOS

No. I don't seem to be. It's the first
I've had a chance to look. A miracle.
I don't see how I avoided it.
Fate has some worse death in store for me.

KALLIOPE

Tarakaia has been wounded.
She is covered with blood.

TARAKAIA

That blood
Is not mine.
I stood in the Hun's tent.
They were weighing out the gold,

She begins to dance.

II CHORUS

The shameful tribute money.

TARAKAIA

Without warning their horns roared.

II CHORUS

Trumpets longer than two men,
That moan like the sea, like death.

TARAKAIA

Horses screamed all around us.

II CHORUS

The great tent swayed in the wind.

All the horde roared like devils,

Like a million devils riding
The sandstorms of the desert.

Soldiers poured into the tent.

If there are extra dancers they enter here.

Through the door we could see
The fires spring up in the city.

Our men began fighting.

Hermaios turned deadly white.

He put his hand over his eyes
And lay back in his chair.

He fainted for a moment.

Then he sprang up and seized his sword.

He began hacking his way
Towards the Hunnish king.

TARAKAIA
I rose.

One of the Second Chorus hands her a sword.

II CHORUS
She took the sword from a man
He had killed.

The hand was still
Twitching.

119

She started to fight.

They were all afraid of her.

They let her kill them like sheep.

Their hot blood covered her face.

TARAKAIA
Their blood blinded my eyes.

II CHORUS
Her hair was clotted with blood.

Their dying hands clutched at her clothes.

They tore the dress from her shoulders.

Blood ran between her breasts.

Hot blood ran down her belly.

TARAKAIA
Thick blood flooded into my womb.

II CHORUS
Her feet slipped in squirming bowels.

She was wonderful,

Naked,
Fiery red with steaming blood.

The sword broke.

One of the Second Chorus hands her a huge axe.

TARAKAIA
  They gave me an axe.

II CHORUS
  Men fell on their knees before her.

  She swung the axe through the air.

  She beheaded them like pigs.

  Fountains of blood gushed over her.

  The Khan turned and ran from her.

  Their princes ran for their lives.

  The extra dancers run out.

  The tent swayed and began to fall.

  Our men cut their way through the walls.

  Outside, the few Greek soldiers
  Were fighting in a hollow square,
  In a heap of dead savages,

  A breastwork higher than a man.

  We fought our way to their horses.

  They all reared when she tried to mount.

  One great white stallion stood for her.

  *One of the Second Chorus hands her a horse, a
  white riding whip.*

  She was beautiful, a naked
  Woman, red with blood, on a white horse.

Tarakaia goes out.

HERMAIOS

We had to fight all the way back
To where the road rises for the mountains.
We had to swim our horses through ice
In the freezing water. I am cold.

DEMETRIOS

Bring the king a cloak.

One of the Second Chorus goes out.

KALLIOPE

Is that all?
There was no warning? Didn't they
Even pretend to offer terms?

HERMAIOS

We parleyed with them for hours. They seemed
To be friendly enough. They wanted
Us to give them double the tribute
And take all of the Greeks and withdraw
To the Roman borders. In exchange
They guaranteed us a thousand
Of their cavalry as an escort.
We could have kept them. They were anxious
To see Rome as our private army.
The chiefs seemed to think they would impress
The Romans. I don't doubt they would have.
After I refused this, they proposed
That we go with them to India.
They knew there are still many Greeks there.

They hoped I could rally them and we
Could all conquer India together.
I said No. I was explaining
That this was not Alexander's day,
Or even Menander's, that the Greeks
Had changed, that the warriors were now monks,
Their women had become prostitutes,
That you can't conquer a continent
With craftsmen and merchants. While we were
Talking I heard the army shouting and moving.
As the guards barred the door of the tent,
I saw the first fires in the city.
There must have been many traitors there.

KALLIOPE

You mean you were offered the chance
To leave with safety and honor
And you refused? You really did that?

*One of the Second Chorus enters with a crimson
cloak for Hermaios.*

HERMAIOS

They killed Julius Caesar for wearing
A thing like this. Of course I refused.

DEMETRIOS

Why?

HERMAIOS

In the first place, I don't think we could
Have crossed Parthia with so many.
But even so, I should have refused.

123

Rome is not my country. This is all
That is left of Greece. I have conquered
And lost far more than Gaul in my day.
I am a better man than Caesar.
Hermaios the Savior, King of Kings,
Of a few cow pastures and mountains.

KALLIOPE

But we will die here, or decay
In squalor and idiocy,
A race of cretins. Had we gone
To Rome we could have been happy
And comfortable and quite rich,
And with our knowledge of the East,
We would have become richer still.

DEMETRIOS

We would certainly be very
Fashionable considering
Our great ancestry and many
Adventures.

KALLIOPE

Oh, we could have had
A wonderful life. As it is
Our race will die out here, ugly
And dirty, cowherds and hotel
Keepers for Chinese traders.

HERMAIOS

So be it. What have I to do
With a world of rhetoricians,

Pederasts and worshippers of Caesar?
Shall I who have held all the countries
Around the moving desert, I who
Have been a terror to the people
In the lands of ice, I who have been
Worshipped as the Destroyer as I
Danced with my beloved in the smoke
In the temples in the jungle, I
Shall now embarrass painted fairies?
Shall I compete with nude actresses
Full of progressive ideas, and with
The inventors of new derangements?
Or shall I import new religions
For millionairesses with rotten
Eyes and cannibal bellies? Shall I,
The last free Greek, make freedom smart
At drunken banquets, almost as smart
As the latest mullet pickle, or
The latest British gladiator?

KALLIOPE

That's not the choice. We could have stayed
In Athens or Alexandria
On our own terms and dignity.
What is life for drunken peasants
Lost in the alleys of midnight,
Staggering in mud and darkness?
You talk of your dignity, you
Have chosen only sordidness.

HERMAIOS

No. It's the Roman world that's sordid.

The Huns have drawn a curtain of blood
And iron between us and the past,
And left us free here to start over.
There is a hundred miles of good
Meadow land in this valley and we
Have the cream of our troops and people.
Only one trail crosses the mountains,
And it's only open in summer.
No one can get up the valley past
The forts at the hot springs. We can make
A perfect city here. Plato's dream,
The City of the Sun, the doomed dream
Of Agis and Cleomenes, we
Can make them all come true in this place.

DEMETRIOS

All of them? Are you sure they aren't
Contradictory?
Forgive me.

HERMAIOS

We are invulnerable and rich
In herds and the gold of three hundred
Years of careful empire. We can wait.
In time we may grow powerful again.
We are better off here. In the city
We had formed habits of luxury.
We had grown careless and forgotten
Our responsibilities and race.
We are sealed away from distraction.
We can give all our energies to
Build a city of brotherly love.

DEMETRIOS

With time and patience mulberry
Leaves may be turned into satin.

HERMAIOS

If we are wise, we will face the fact
That we have ceased to have any part
In history.

DEMETRIOS

At least it is
More prudent to wait. Sometimes you
Can force fortune by withdrawing
From all action.

HERMAIOS

History begins
When the family sickens with conflict
And flies apart.

DEMETRIOS

Fortune, like most
Disasters, exercises her
Power only when we oppose
No obstacles to her progress.

HERMAIOS

History ends in death.

DEMETRIOS

Fortune
Is only changeable to those
Who can't or won't adapt themselves.

HERMAIOS

At the end the virtuous and wise
Pass beyond history to a new
Family of love and devotion.

DEMETRIOS

Men are thrown into prominence
By circumstances that match their
Characters. History has both
Very rash and prudent moments.

HERMAIOS

The actions of men move in cycles.
The gods never do the same thing twice.

DEMETRIOS

Few men can really change themselves
With the wavering moods of time.
One time—we conquer High Asia,
Another—we save what we can.
There is not much use in watching
A stake against which a running
Hare struck its head and died. It may
Be some time before another
Hare happens to come along. I
Think it prudent to know when to yield.

KALLIOPE

I see no point in your prudence.
There is no praise that has not been
Lavished on prudence, yet she can't
Insure the most trifling event.

And furthermore, you can't escape
From history with dignity.
History crosses the beggar's
Palm and squeezes through the whore's womb.
Your fine dreams are impractical.
You live in a world of your own.
Look around you—where are the wise
And virtuous? Not amongst us.

DEMETRIOS

I agree with the king. You said
The Huns offered us a thousand
Horsemen?

HERMAIOS

Yes.

DEMETRIOS

Were they to supply themselves?

HERMAIOS

I imagine so. There's no way we could.

DEMETRIOS

They'd bring their wagons and people.
We would be about three thousand.
That's not enough and too many.
Not enough to beat off any
Attack, too many to avoid
Notice. We'd simply be turned back
By the Parthians. No nation
Would allow such a horde trooping

129

Across it. I suppose after
They tire of looting the city
They would still be willing to go?

HERMAIOS

Oh, yes, there is no doubt about it.
They were more anxious to go with us
To Rome than to stay with their own king.

DEMETRIOS

It is probably wiser, and
Certainly far more noble to stay,
As it is more noble to choose
A greater good than a lesser evil.

HERMAIOS

I am glad you agree with me. I
Have done only what I had to do.

*Tarakaia enters, her hair dressed, and in a black,
draped cloth, like the white ones of Hermaios and
the beggar.*

DEMETRIOS

That is all any of us do.

KALLIOPE

I do not see this greater good.
It seems to me I've heard you say
That politics is the art of
Choosing the lesser evil—but
I bow my woman's wilfullness
To my brother's and husband's will.

DEMETRIOS

You cannot explain politics
To a woman except in terms
Of her morals or her feelings.
This is the reason why the Greeks
Grew lightheaded in old age
And were smashed by a young nation
With neither feelings nor morals.

KALLIOPE

You contradict yourself.

DEMETRIOS

I don't.
A new era begins tonight.

He gestures, aside, to Kalliope.

You, get ready for sacrifice
A black heifer and a white bull.

He speaks to one of the Second Chorus.

KALLIOPE

Your bath is ready. Will you come in?

HERMAIOS

I should not wear this purple robe. I
Have never been guilty of such pride
In my life. It is a bad omen.

KALLIOPE

Nonsense. It will be off in the bath,
And then you will be clothed in the white

Robes of a priest. Now you are a king
Taking rule over a new empire.

She ties a diadem around his head.

HERMAIOS

No.
Doubt overcomes me. I may be wrong.
I hope I made the right decision.
I may have made a fatal mistake.
I can no longer see ahead
For the smoke and the mist.
I am clouded over with doubt.
When we think we are at our best, we
May be steered by a lifetime's evils.

DEMETRIOS

Crime is a tribute paid to life.
When the heart trembles, we still it
With ritual. Will you go in?

*Demetrios, Kalliope, and Hermaios go out, leaving
Tarakaia standing, rigid and silent, in the center of
the stage.*

II CHORUS

My blood ran cold to hear them
Chaffer quotations like that.

I doubt if they were aware
Of it. Like deeds bring like words.

Do you think the king really
Has no idea of what is
About to happen to him?

I think he has a very
Accurate estimate
Of the immediate future.

I CHORUS

The acts of men move in endless
Recurrent cycles. The heavens
Never do quite the same thing twice.

Tarakaia begins the faintest suggestion of a dance.

The equinoxes close their term.
The planets line up once again
At the post, but the drifting stars
Of the Great Bear have formed a cart
To haul a king to the scaffold.

Kalliope enters.

KALLIOPE

Will you come in? You are the priestess.
The bath is waiting. The altar
Is being made ready for you.
The axe is ready and the noose,
And the victims are being bathed.
I have brought you a wreath to wear.

*She throws a wreath of large white roses over Tara-
kaia's neck.*

II CHORUS

I do not like those roses.

They look like a wreath of skulls.

TARAKAIA

Soon. I will come in right away.
Let me stand just a moment
And watch the snow blowing across
The mountains. Then I will come in.

KALLIOPE

I shall wait for you in the bath.

She goes out.

TARAKAIA

She is right. If you have a sword
In your heart, you should take it out
And use it. But she is afraid.
She is more afraid than we are.

1 CHORUS

Jealousy blinds the eyes of love
With a darkness full of deathly
Fear.

TARAKAIA

The queen and Demetrios
Are all alone. They cannot find
And touch each other in the dark
And cold of their loneliness.

1 CHORUS

We
See the world lit by each other.

The damned burn, not with want of love,
But with the wish to be loved alone.

Hoarded love is a cold cancer.

The miser of love dies alone,
A dog in a manger of black
Fire in an empty universe.

Such love touches men's bowels with death,
And gives body to disaster.
Even now her fear hands a sword
To the guilt that shall avenge her.

A red bath shall be her childbed.
She feeds an armed man in her womb.

TARAKAIA

Let her alone.
See how the snow . . .

*She begins to dance very slowly. During the dance
the Second Chorus hand her a small axe and a noose.*

I CHORUS

Is a fine haze in the moonlight.

The wind blows it back and forth like
A sheer gauze curtain.

The mountain
Comes and goes, vast, indefinite.

The pass is black in the shadow.
Beyond, over Tibet, the storm
Is coming, dry and dead,
Violent, with no snow in it.

Murderous cold and blackness boil
There in the clear midwinter night.

Demons ride around in the whirlwind,
Spinning like the shells of dead sins,
The insect casts of squalid lives.

The dead grass is blown from its roots.

Cattle whimper in the dark barns.

The winter birds are blown away.

Under the rocks, curled like unborn
Children, the coneys sleep in their
Grass nests.

The stars are pitiless.
The stone desert is without end.

TARAKAIA

One summer we crossed those mountains
Laughing through the tall blue poppies.

I CHORUS

Now the jewel-eyed spotted bears
Stumble blinded with cold into
The houses and are killed with clubs.

In the drifted meadows the fox
Strangles and sinks from sight in the snow.

The eagle and lamb are frozen
In midair and fall through the wind.

Their red blood mingles and smokes like
Fire on the black rocks and white snow.

In the middle of the whirling,
Screaming triangles of the storm,
A minute eye of light opens.

He stands in the pitching cyclone,
He who hears the world's cry, he who
Listens to the sound of being,
His dark bride growing from his reins.

One of the Second Chorus comes in.

II CHORUS

    The queen has sent me for you.
I do not like to do this—
But it is my job. If I
Don't do it, someone else will.
Come. I don't believe in force.

She gives him a ring.

TARAKAIA

    This ring is for Berenike.
Be sure to see that she gets it.
It is a star sapphire. They say
It was Helen's ring once, in Troy.
Here, you can keep everything else.

She gives him all her jewelry.

II CHORUS

    I must obey orders.

TARAKAIA

I know.
I suppose you love your children.
As I watch the fierce stars shining
On all the twisting roads of pain,
I know it is not I alone,
Caught in the freezing of the year.

I CHORUS

The bliss of supernatural
Calm and the trouble and turmoil
Of grasping and losing are but
The knuckles and palm of one hand,
That touches the earth in languor.

Reality is a whirling sphere
Whose center and circumference
Continuously are becoming
Each other.

*She speaks to the First Chorus, who come forward in
this last scene; all have their backs to the audience,
facing the closed screen, except the Second Chorus
(guard), who is in quarter face to profile, looking over
his shoulder at Tarakaia as he goes toward the door.*

TARAKAIA

Are you comforting
Me? I don't need such deep visions.
Help me. I am weak and afraid.
I have been loved by a great king.
Wizards and strong men have feared me.
Tonight as the sun set over

The stormy mountains, I killed men.
I have marched across the haunted
Sand, and through jungles filled with leeches
With Hermaios. Am I now
Afraid to walk after him through
A door? Let go.
Pah! •

She starts forward and spits.

II CHORUS
Why do you spit?

TARAKAIA
I smell the odor of my death
In front of my body.

She speaks to the First Chorus.

You're wise,
Did it ever occur to you
That if the mountains gave us strength
To carry them, we should carry
A large mountain more easily
Than a small one, because a large
Mountain would give us the more strength?

She goes out.

*After a pause, there is a hoarse cry from Hermaios,
then a short, siren-like wail from Tarakaia. Another
pause, and the bodies are exposed in the doorway,
lying on the crimson robe, Demetrios and Kalliope
standing right and left. Demetrios begins a speech.*

DEMETRIOS

My friends. . . .

Berenike enters, at the left, stealthily.

BEYOND THE MOUNTAINS

II—Berenike

BERENIKE

The scene is the same as before, except that the light is dimmer and more blue. The inner wings of the rear screen open back and reveal the catafalques of Hermaios and Tarakaia. These are dummies or bolsters, with the masks, lying on portable camp beds and completely draped, Hermaios with his red cloak, Tarakaia with her black one. An overhead white or very pale yellow light, quite dim, shines from directly above on them. Just behind the right rear member of the Second Chorus is a black cylinder pierced with irregular holes, through which a dim red light shines. It represents a "salamander" such as workmen warm themselves by. Berenike, completely covered with a black robe, sits huddled beside it, her head between her knees. The costumes are the same except that over them all the characters wear large squares of black cloth as robes, except Kalliope, who wears white. The swords used by Berenike and Menander are very bright, their effect depending on their brilliant reflection. The head is crudely carved and painted, possibly from balsa wood; it has a tuft of hair by which it can be held. The Huns are dressed as before. A very weak spotlight can be used where necessary, as the general lighting should grow steadily dimmer. The spot on Berenike's sword dance can be moderately bright. Revolving lights of

orange and green can be used for the Huns' dance; if
this is done, the new First Chorus should sit within
the white light which shines throughout on the cata-
falques. Berenike wears the glittering ring which Tara-
kaia gave to the Chorus.

I Chorus

> The wind in the mountains has stopped.
> The silence comes back like a thought.
>
> The frozen water is still,
> But the pulsating moonlight
> Makes ripples in the clear ice.
>
> Haunted by consequence, all
> Existence is uneasy.
>
> There is no reason why a thing
> Should move unless it is able
> To reach the end of its movement.
>
> Man is the only animal
> Who knows he must die.
>
> The spectres
> Of the living pursue the
> Emanations of the dead.

II Chorus

> Why do we have to wake here
> All night in the bitter cold?
> What are we guarding?

The dead.

Much better they guarded us.

It's bitter cold. They'll not spoil
Tonight.

They'll keep a long time.

Longer than Egypt's mummies,
If you ask me.

What did you
Think of Demetrios' speech?

He had something when he said
It was better that one man
Die for the good of many
Than that many perish for
The good of the State.

I think
A good many will perish
Before we ever see Rome.

We will not get away.

Demetrios has nothing
To offer they cannot take
Without asking him for help.

He has many devices.
He can lead them to Rome.

They have only to point their
Horses west and keep chopping.
They don't need his devices.

If Menander should come back,
The whole picture would be changed.

*Menander enters and stands silently at the extreme
left.*

They will break him as they broke
Berenike, cowering
There by the fire.

He won't break.

They can break anybody.

That white devil will make him
Confess he killed his father.

Power can do anything.

You're too sure of their power.
How do you know she's broken?

All I hope is that they have
Power enough to save us.

We're doomed. Hermaios was right.

We are safe bottled up here.
If the Huns get past the gates
Of the forts at the hot springs
In the throat of the valley,
They will exterminate us.

I hope they are well guarded.

That is what we're here to watch.
As long as their beacon shines,
They are all right.

I wish we
Were down there where it's warmer.

Who is he?

Where'd he come from?

Somebody got past the gates.

Menander speaks to the First Chorus.

MENANDER
Is that the body of the king?

I CHORUS
Yes. One of them was once the king,
The other was an Indian witch.

Now they have become something else.

Two infants, two newborn dead in
Their fragile cradles of thin bone.

The kingship has passed to his son.

When he was made prince they called him
Menander, the Guardian God.

MENANDER
I thought Demetrios was king.

I CHORUS
He is of that opinion, too.

MENANDER
Do you know where Menander is?

147

I CHORUS

He is lost in the labyrinth
Of history.

MENANDER

Do you think so?
He may be nearer than you think,
And his fate may be more certain.

I CHORUS

He is further from you than you
Think, and there is little question
About his destiny.

History
Is definite and sure enough.
It is only blind and twisted
To its victims and instruments.

MENANDER

It seems to me like a writhing
Corridor of darkness, a black
Elastic labyrinth.

I CHORUS

I know.
You do not have much perspective
When you are being digested.

MENANDER

Do you know who I am?

I CHORUS

Of course.
You are the last king of the Greeks.
You stand shuddering on the bank
Of the frozen stream of vengeance.

MENANDER

You know more than I.

I CHORUS

That is right.

Living, man does not know his soul.
Dead, he does not know his body.

MENANDER

If you are so wise, then tell me,
What will become of all of us?
What can I know? What must I do?
What can I hope?

I CHORUS

Little enough.
You will do what you have to do.

There is an end to the fingers
That feed the twigs to the fire.
But the fire passes on. No one
Can know when it will be put out.

Act. All things are made new by fire.

149

MENANDER

You talk about the fire of act.
I feel as though I were freezing.
It is all I can do to move
My eyes and lips, let alone act.
I can see all of the future
Under those cloths of red and black.

I CHORUS

Action and inaction are as real
As the swinging clapper of a bell.

Berenike rises.

You will find the source of motion.
You are the ghost of many men.

MENANDER

I do not have it now. I feel
As though I were turning to stone,
A stone in a fog of evil.

Berenike crosses to Menander very slowly.

I CHORUS

The evils of the world are the
Reflexions of the owner of
That world. He chose that special strand,
Out of the infinite webbed globe
Of choice and possibility.

BERENIKE

Who are you?

Menander does not answer.

Are you my brother?
What is wrong with you?
Speak to me.

MENANDER

Are you my sister?
Yes, you are.
Touch me.
Something breathed upon me
Out of the darkness. I am not
Sure any longer who I am.
The horrible brute flood of fate
Flows through my brain like a river
Of moving stones.

BERENIKE

Menander.
We are all that's left. We must be
Everything to each other now.
You are my brother and father,
Mother, son, lover and husband.
I will do anything you want.

MENANDER

I want nothing, and least of all
The burden of other's kinship.
I would much rather be my own
Ancestors and descendants.

151

BERENIKE

What will happen? What can we do?

MENANDER

As wisdom and beauty just said,
We will do what we have to do.
That is all we can ever do.
The question is, what will be done
To us?

BERENIKE

They stripped me and flogged me
Till I fainted. I found myself
Naked and bleeding in the snow.
The soldiers brought this cloak for me
And let me sit by their fire. Look,
I am still bleeding.

She holds open the cloak.

MENANDER

Hide your flesh.
It dazzles me. He said I would
Find the source of motion somewhere.
Can you keep the sword in my hand?

BERENIKE

I want Demetrios myself.
All you have to do is find out
The glass ball that serves for a heart
Hidden in that white, twisting flesh.
It will be like killing a swan.
Her face is dead like a swan's face.

MENANDER

You know we are made of that flesh.

BERENIKE

Not I. Hate has transmuted me.
Bodies migrate from soul to soul
On the flooded streams of passion.

MENANDER

I cannot move. Her bowels
Tangle my feet.

BERENIKE

Your eyes play tricks on you.
Her life sows your pathway with snakes.
What are you standing on now? Think.
Consider where you will step next.
As long as she lives you are poised
On a needle's point in an abyss.

MENANDER

I am suspended on a rope
Of blood.

BERENIKE

You can no longer tell
Up from down nor hard from soft, nor
Your feet from your head. It is
The iron of her will which holds you
Spitted like a lark over the
Vacant fires of nothingness.

MENANDER

I cannot move. If I were to move
My hand an inch towards my sword
A million voices would cry out
In all the corridors of my blood.

BERENIKE

Those are not corridors of blood,
But black alleyways of nothing.
You do not live in being but
In the holes chopped in it by fate—
The gapes of doom, the eaten child,
The lust of the inhuman swan.

MENANDER

But it is you who cry vengeance.
You are the voice of consequence,
The automatic damnation
Of our aged blood. It is you
Who are snarled in the web of cause.
I only want to turn no more
On the turning wheels.

BERENIKE

You are blind.
The door to inaction is called
Action, and the gate of action
Is called inaction. You cannot
Find bliss by dropping your eyelids.
Some are moved by others. Some move
Others. Some move themselves. Some are
Immobile. So men are graded.

You have not even begun
To climb this ladder. Another
Holds you fast in her own dreaming.
Spitted or strangled, you are fixed;
You are not yet a human being.
At birth you free your own navel
With your own hands, and claim the six
Directions of space for yourself.

MENANDER

You do not move me. It is you
Who wants me in your burning dream.
You want to make a tool of me.
You want vengeance because you loved
My father. You loved his mistress,
And loved him doubled so as in
A mirror. You coiled between their
Loving bellies like a kitten
In bed, like an egg in the nest.
At last they came to love each other
Only across the bridge of you.
You were their sexual organ.
Now you bridge nothing to nothing.
The queen and her brother fear you.
They have always feared you. If you
Could creep between them in their bed
You would forget about revenge.
I never loved my father, but
I know my duty and my fate.
They shall be complete, I suppose,
But I shall not will them. My acts
Will be only images of acts.

The shadow falls on the sundial,
The column drops in the waterclock,
The stars blaze out and fall to earth,
Without good or evil or consent.

*Menander and Berenike begin to dance, slowly and
with little movement. The first climax is still some
time ahead.*

I CHORUS
She has conquered him and he thinks
He is denying her.

Passion
Floods her. She swings like a lodestone.

Her white body and her vast eyes
Glow like rubbed amber in the dark.

Little fires run over her hair.

She is only an empty box
Whose walls are action and passion.

She is nothing, but she can hold
Persons, things, beginnings and ends.

II CHORUS
How beautiful the princess looks
In spite of everything.

She looks beautiful but tired.

I think she looks bored but weak.

No. Weary but determined.

I think she looks hot, specially
When she looks at her brother.

If she looked at me like that
I wouldn't know what to do.

Their faces are together.
They look exactly alike.

I used to think she looked like
The Indian girl, but really
She looks just like Menander.

They look like each other.

Son,
Profound thoughts cross your mind.

Well, it's the truth, isn't it?

They pause in the dance.

BERENIKE
You think I want to use you. No.
I want you to use me. Use me,
All of me, till I am used up,
Until there is nothing left of me,
Only you and your action.
Only your will. I want to be
Like a straw cart loaded with fire,
A vehicle which perishes
As it runs. I am yours to burn.

MENANDER
There is no judgment without fire.

157

There is no fire without judgment.
I have passed discrimination.
I judge nothing. I shall not act.
I shall only suffer action
To take place. You will find no fire
In me.

BERENIKE

Your being judges me.
You need do nothing but exist
To judge me and so create me.
If I am close to your being,
If I sheathe your acts in passion,
I am close to the fire. If I
Am far from you, I am far from
Judgment.

MENANDER

I have no real being.
I am like an astronomer's
Imaginary line, just one
Probable strand in your cobweb
Of the infinite possible,
And so are you to me. Millions
Times millions Menanders
Face the unending mirrors of
Berenikes at this instant,
And a million times a million
Berenikes see themselves in
The firelit pupils of their brothers,
As I see myself in your eyes.

Fire lights the image and the eye.
The winter cold drinks up the fire.

BERENIKE

I am the bow-drill, the tinder,
The sweet cedar sticks, the incense.
The fire comes from you, from your heart.
When it flames I am your image
Reflected in the glassy flame,
And your vast shadow on the dark.

I CHORUS

All things are made new by fire.

From
The one to the two, from the
Two to the many, from the many
To the not many, from the not
Many to the not two, from the
Not two to the not one.

The snake
Of is and is not eats himself.

He feels himself become one.

Alone in his own being
He joys in exaltation.

In the husk of forgetting
Grows the seed of memory.

He selfs himself beyond himself.

He sees himself in his own eyes.

Snow falls in water.

Fire drinks fire.

Grass has the grass for companion.

The serpent gives birth to the bull.

The bull gives birth to the serpent.

The star of wonder rises and
No one hinders it, for it is
Concluded of in the counsels
Of the watchmen in the gates of
The deep.

Love slays what they have been.
And they become what they were not.

Each spirit eats its own body,
Out of passion into action.

The hunger of time eats of time.
The hunger of eternity
Eats of eternity.

They are
The magic of the eternal
Lust, the lust of the eternal
Magic.

*Berenike draws Menander's sword, dances with it,
and then hands it to him. As she does so, an identical
sword appears in her hand. Soon he gives her his,
and she dances with both, running, posturing, and
whirling the swords with increasing rapidity. At the*

*climax she is enveloped in a sphere of glassy light,
the reflection of the whirling swords. At this moment
the spotlight shifts from her to just above his head,
where a sword appears, brilliantly lit, held aloft, up-
right, as high as he can reach.*

Lightning whirls on the peak.

The god dances, the flute player.

The goddess dances, with two swords.

Curtains of fire creep in the sky.

Fire dragons couple in heaven.

The god dances, the king of the dance.

The goddess dances, queen of lust.

The world is a globe of lightning.

Cobwebs of lightning fill all space.

The moon marries the sun, vast clouds
Of lightning burst from their wedding.

Nets of lightning whirl from her womb.

A ring of fiery blood blossoms
Around them and closes them in.

The transparent moon falls away.

The sun springs forth from blazing blood.

A pillar of fire burns on the mountain.

A musette sounds.

II CHORUS
Demetrios! Demetrios!

Menander, his sword in his hand (Berenike's have vanished) steps behind the screen. Demetrios, with an identical sword, held in the same position, enters from the left.

Long life!
        Long life!
                Long life!
                        Long life!

DEMETRIOS
An unknown man has been reported,
Wrapped in a black cloak that beats like wings,
Along the road between here and the gates.
Have you seen him? Did he pass this way?

I CHORUS
No one is here but the dead king.

No one has come but the living.

Only the princess, embracing
The fire.

DEMETRIOS
No one unknown?

I CHORUS
No one.

DEMETRIOS

My girl, have you seen anybody?

He speaks very self-consciously.

BERENIKE

Only a man I love.

DEMETRIOS

What are you
Talking about? Who is this person?

BERENIKE

He is afraid of me. It is hard
To give myself to him. He fears
To act. Fate points to a woman
And he struggles to evade her.
He does not seem to realize
That he is all powerful. If
He would act, I would be queen.

DEMETRIOS

Who is this you are talking about?

She comes close to him.

BERENIKE

They say he is the last Greek king.
I love him beyond all the world.
He never knew it until now.

DEMETRIOS

I don't believe you. You're mocking me.

BERENIKE

Touch me. Put your hand on my breasts.

DEMETRIOS

Your heart beats like thunder. A swooning
Shivering lightning pours from your breast.
It grips my hand. I cannot move it.

BERENIKE

You touch my breasts, now you can guess
The power of the lust for you
That roars and shakes deep inside me,
Until it blinds and deafens me.

DEMETRIOS

Why have you waited to tell me this?

BERENIKE

This is the opportune moment.
Circumstance has kept me silent.
At last I can offer you freedom,
More absolute than you can hope.
She falters and dreams and hangs back.
Here is all my youth, its blood and
Deep oblivion. Once you are caught
Between these thighs you will be free
In a different universe.
Only you can fill my hunger.
Only I can cut your bonds.
Do you know what it will be like
To lie between my legs? You will
Cease to be as Demetrios.

164

I will change you to another
Order of being. There is fire
Inside me will set you aflame
Like incense on an altar.

DEMETRIOS

Slowly. Slowly. My head whirls as if
It would leave my shoulders. This is the
Last thing in the world I expected.

BERENIKE

You are right. You have never looked
For life to offer you any
Finality. My father chose
One absolute. He tried to freeze
Time in its passing. My mother
Can only give you the idle
Comfort of a few Roman years.
You do not know what burns in me.
Time will perish for you in my arms.

She opens her cloak.

Your whip made these marks.
They only make my lust stronger.
Each time I think of you they all
Cry out for you like famished wombs.

DEMETRIOS

Clothe yourself. I fall. There is nothing
To stop me falling infinitely.

II CHORUS

The queen.

BERENIKE

Get rid of my mother.
Quickly. I cannot wait too long.
Be quick. I will consume myself.

She runs out.

DEMETRIOS

I have seen an hallucination.
My brother's death has disorganized
My brain. There was no girl here, only
My sick conscience shaped like a hot whore.
If I do not watch myself, my guilt
Will open gulfs of lust and despair
At my feet and swallow me alive.
I was staring in a blazing hole—
The pit of oblivion masked as the
Swoon of love. I could see my brother
Standing between the lips of her sex
Like a ghost in a fiery furnace.

He tries to speak casually.

Have you seen the princess recently?

I CHORUS

No one has moved across this stage
Tonight but the marionettes
Of choice and consequence.

No one but the impassive dead
Who act without motion.

Demetrios waves his hand before his eyes and shakes his head.

II CHORUS
The queen.

Kalliope enters.

DEMETRIOS
Are you all right? How do you feel?

KALLIOPE
Sick.
Cold. Are the valley gates secure?

DEMETRIOS
They were closed tight and strongly guarded.
I don't think the Huns can get through them.
But something else might. On the cliff road
The men have seen strange figures beyond
The light of their bivouacs, which vanished
When challenged. I saw some dark wing'd form
Wavering before me just as I got here.
Then there was a burning animal
Shaped like a naked girl. I knew her.
She came out of my own distraction.
I must get some rest and peace. My skull
Is full of black eels crawling like fire.
But cold and black. I am very tired.

KALLIOPE
I am freezing. Every minute
Is colder than the last. Just now

When I looked into my mirror
My breath froze until I
Could not see my face anymore.
Where my image should have answered
Me there was only a blank disc
Of crystal ice. This cold is like
A hand of bone. It probes in me.
It reaches deeper and deeper,
Into my bowels, hunting for the
Secret flame at the root of my
Spine. There is hardly anything left
Of that flame now. The years have used
Almost all of its fuel. Soon
That creeping hand will touch it with
Cold bone and it will go out.
I cannot last much longer. We
Must try to leave this place tonight.
Do you hear me? When can we leave?

DEMETRIOS

I was thinking about something else.
I sent Eucratides to the Khan
To tell him we accepted his terms.
He should be back in the next hour.
I wonder what it will be like in Rome?
There was a Roman in India
When I was there. He was very rich.
All his body servants were black girls.
They went naked and their skin glistened
Like wet frogs. He spent most of his time
Being massaged while they read obscene
Novels to him. But my equerry

168

Saw him kill a tiger with his fist.
He baited tigers with his black girls,
And used only a short sword on them.
Romans have terrible appetites.
They say Julius dressed like a woman.
They say Lucullus fed Panthea
The roast flesh of young men. I wonder
What it will be like in Rome? There are
No mountains there like these. There are mountains,
Though, the Alps. Hannibal had trouble . . .

KALLIOPE

Are you sure that Eucratides
Will return by midnight? Perhaps
The Khan will not see him so late.

DEMETRIOS

He will see him. I wish I were young
Again. I dread starting life over
Again in a strange place. I would like
To go to an island in some warm sea
And sleep and eat, and drowse in the arms
Of a childish girl. For a thousand
Miles in any direction there is
Nothing tonight but sandstorms and ice,
Ignorant armies that clash in dark,
And blood that freezes as it spills.

KALLIOPE

Hark.
I heard something moving out there.

DEMETRIOS

It is a bat that walks like a man.
Or a hot beast with the breasts and sex
Of a crazy girl.

A round object falls into the circle of light.

KALLIOPE

What is that?
Good god, what is it? Pick it up.
No. Don't touch it. It might be alive.

*He picks it up and holds it towards her. She screams
and runs out.*

DEMETRIOS

It is not alive. It is the head
Of Eucratides. He looks surprised.
I guess he wasn't expecting it.
It's too bad that everything is more
Complex than death. There's something
Almost comic about its simplicity.
I guess that's what surprised him. He was
A hero and looked for something grand.
The world's a tragedy to those who
Feel, a comedy to those who think.
And that is all for Eucratides.

He throws the head over the cliff. Kalliope returns.

KALLIOPE

Where is it? What did you do with it?

DEMETRIOS

What?

KALLIOPE

The head of Eucratides.

DEMETRIOS

Is it missing? Poor Eucratides.
Brave, but inclined to lose his head.
Rash, really, I'd say, rather than brave.

KALLIOPE

It was here a moment ago.

DEMETRIOS

Eucratides' head?

KALLIOPE

You know it was.
The Huns cut it off and threw it
At our feet. Right there in the dark
Hunnish warriors laugh at us.

DEMETRIOS

Hallucinations, my soft sweetheart,
Not as nice as the honey dripping
Hallucination there in your crotch,
But unreal, very unreal. Believe
Nothing tonight. See no evil, hear
No evil, speak no evil. Leave me.

He sits down abruptly in the center of the step be-tween the First Chorus.

171

I must think. Thought's more complex than death.
It's a sort of intermittent
Foxfire of the dark quaking heart.

Kalliope stares at him and goes out.

She's gone and that football with its teeth
And stony eyes is gone. The black man
Is gone. Watch. The little naked one
Will come back.

Berenike steps from behind the screen.

BERENIKE

I have never left.
What are you going to do now?
You have nowhere to turn now
Except to me. Come to me. Look.
Look at me. I am ready for you.

She lies on the floor with her knees lifted and spread.

DEMETRIOS

Go away. You distract me. Vanish.
I want to think. Soon I will be dead.
The dead are too simple to think much.
Stop bothering me and go away.
The situation is new to me.
I don't know what to do about it.

BERENIKE

Come to me. Come to me quickly.
I am grovelling before you.
I can no longer see or hear.

All the world roars and turns red.
Drop your sword and fall into me.
Fill me. Satisfy me. I burn.
Now. This instant. I burn like fire.
Come. Come. Cover me with death.

She screams, a long, wailing scream. Demetrios rises, whirls around, his sword drops beside her. As he falls stiffly upon her, she, screaming, runs him through.

DEMETRIOS

Death. Life. Wings. Beasts. Kings. Wombs. Blood.
  Swords.

You're a very clever child.

It's true.
The spasm of love and the spasm
Of death are much alike. Both spasms.

He dies.

BERENIKE

What a simple soul. Help me up.

She raises herself on her elbows and pushes him away. The Second Chorus places him between Hermaios and Tarakaia.

How easy it was, like testing
Pudding. Menander will not have
So easy a time. She'll die hard.
Poor beef, did I hate you so short
A moment ago? Now I feel

173

All hollowed out. If my mother
Appeared now I would be tempted
To let her escape.

II Chorus
Menander.

Berenike

Soon it will be over, our own
Private tale of hate and ruin,
And the long story of the Greeks.
All that orderly, musical,
Curious world will never be
Again. And our sour trickle
Of Alexander's blood will seep
Out forever in desert sand.
New love. New death,
My sweet brother.

*She staggers a little as Menander enters, grips his
hand and leans heavily against him.*

Menander
What is wrong?

Berenike
I am exhausted.
Hold me for a moment. Kiss me.
It's like kissing the evening star.
I'm corrupt and you're very pure.
You are like sweet running water.
Are you ready?

174

MENANDER

Yes, I'm ready.
What do you want?

BERENIKE

Demetrios
Is dead.

She points. Menander looks at him in silence for a while.

MENANDER

He seems to be with friends.
They get along with each other.
I doubt if he is powerful
As they are, but at least he acts
One single-minded deed to add
His force to this dry debacle.
Life's simple appetites meant much
To all of them. I wish I could
Touch them and say, "Live, run away,
Hide in the mountains. For thirty
Years you can eat mutton and loll
Beside meadow streams blowing
Grass whistles at the passing clouds."

BERENIKE

He who buys a dried fish so that
He can set it free, does not know
The distinctions of life and death.

MENANDER

He said, "The one for the good of

175

Many is higher than many
For the good of all, as the death
Of heroes is nobler than the
Waste of spawning salmon," and now
He is just dead, ignobly dead,
But indistinguishable from
Hermaios, that noble hero.
Lesser evil and greater good.
I wonder if either of them
Expected death to be so simple.
One more to go. This is almost
The end of all of us. I think
We were doomed by an empty whim
Of the passionate gods whose vain
Frivolities disturb the order
Of men. What will we gain at last?
The good side of the coin says, "King
Of Kings, the Savior God." The bad
Side says, "Fifty Cents."

BERENIKE

Do you hang
Back again? Have you forgotten
That love gave you the power to act?

MENANDER

I do not act. There are some believe
Translucent bodies in heaven
Cast invisible shadows in
Which our bodies move.

BERENIKE

You sank into
My flesh as the eye falls through
The doubled mirrors that retreat
Forever. This is the will's source,
Not the mathematics of heaven.

MENANDER

My will? I have as many wills
As a tree has branches and twigs.
Each act is an acorn from which
There hangs an oak of choice into
Space—from the fiery earth into
Black space, from the black earth into
Fiery space.

BERENIKE

No. Act grows from will.
Will grows from love. Look in your sword.
The sword is the perfect mirror
Of naked love.

She presses her belly.

Here is the source
Of all our outrageous deeds
As we live each other's death and
Die each other's life.

MENANDER

Your hungry
Womb? My leathery heart? Those sprouting
Acorns of necessity?

BERENIKE

Love,
Somewhere you and I are stars, here
We live in these trivial things,
Two human hearts ruled by desire
And necessity.

MENANDER

The heavens
Can be invoked with confidence.
They are empty and will not heed
Our importunities. No vast
Celestial machinery
Moves us through night to doom, no star
Shines in heaven and in my heart.
Somewhere hidden in the last
Recesses of being is a little
Machine, a little engine
That runs the whole thing. It is a
Little bit of a thing. You could
Hold it in your hand. I don't think
It is very complex, something
Simple, just a few wheels and valves.
It all depends on that, the whole
Universe. And it is going
To tick away there forever
Unless someone finds and destroys it.

BERENIKE

We must act beyond necessity.

MENANDER

My dear love. Your dreams of action
Are dreams of one who dreams he dreams.
Take me in your arms. I leave you
Now. Forever and forever.

BERENIKE

What do you mean? Where are you going?

MENANDER

At the other end of the universe
There is another Menander
And another Berenike.
We have hunted them all our lives.
At last tonight we will meet them.

I CHORUS

That is what the universe
Is.

The thing that hangs between
Those doubled figures.

BERENIKE

Forever.

Menander goes out with drawn sword.

I CHORUS

Time is enclosed in
Forever as in a box and
All the forevers are enclosed

179

In Eternity like the seeds
In a pomegranate.

The past is shut in the present,
The present closed in the future.

Time is a series of boxes,
One closed in the other. In the
Last box is a tiny image
Of the god of comedy, the
Only begettor of them all,
The father of the great false gods,
The Past, The Present, The Future.

BERENIKE

At last the fruit of deed is ripe.
The golden apple, consequence,
Is about to drop from the tree.

*She begins to dance, very slowly, and, as it were,
inconspicuously at first.*

I CHORUS

All action rises in the heart.

Every deed begins there, runs its
Course in the tangle of the world,

Comes to final fruition there.

Suffering follows on thought and act
As the wheel follows the ox's hoof.

Out of every act a person
Appears. From acts without strength
Come cripples, monsters, and the blind.

From irresponsible actions
Come insensate conspiracies,

The kingdoms of men, their power,
And history's bastard image
Of time's breaking, falling mirrors.

We act in the world of illusion
Where action is busy with means.
In the world of reality
The single act is its own end.

In every particle of dust
There are Troys without number, Troys
Where the Greeks won and where they lost,
And countless Helens who never
Left home, or who died in peace on
Phrygian thrones.

There are countless
Iphigenias marching to
Their deaths at this moment in all
The dust motes of the rising sun.

There are no things in the real
World. Only persons have being.
Things are perspectives on persons—
A mote of dust is a distant
Person seen with dusty interest.

The dance takes definition here.

Light falls through the empty heaven.

Stars drift and rock on the waves of time.

The transparent earth curdles to stone.

Light floods the rock. Water is born
From stone. Air springs from the wave's spray.
Fire kindles in the light-filled air.

Light curdles in the virgin womb.

The earth turns to a crystal ball.
The child is at the gates. The waves
Of the endless sea grow still.

Light
Shines, a perfect disc reflected
In infinite calm.

Light narrows
To a point.

The point of light gives birth
To an illimitable sphere
Of rainbows flowing forever.

The dance closes during the next six lines.

II CHORUS

The star climbs near the zenith.
Soon it will stand above them,
Where they wait in the desert.

The whirling equinoxes
Close their term.

The Great Year ends.

The heavens begin again.
But we will not begin.

Time
Is all gone for the Greeks now.

She stands gazing at the bodies.

Just think, we might have fallen
At Thermopylae, or seen
The cherry blooming by the sea
With Xenophon, or have died
Sick in looted Babylon
With Alexander, or talked
Of love and death and the Soul,
And sunk in cool oblivion
With Socrates, or fell at Troy.
And here we are, witnesses
Of the last Greek hours.

She goes out.

The last
Greek minutes.

I wonder if
Plato and Aristotle
In all their wisdom foresaw
Greece ending in these far-off
Mountains, in this freezing night?

In Sparta and Athens now,
The Roman slave refines his wit;

Not one subtle gentleman
Will ever hear that we are gone.

No monument will mark us.

One of the Second Chorus rises and carves some-
thing with his knife on the right screen. He steps
back and another looks over his shoulder and reads.

What are you doing?

What has he written?

"Stranger, when you
Come to Lakadaimon, tell
Them we lie here, obedient
To their will."

Forever.

From this point on the Second Chorus ignore the
other actors. They drink, talk, sing softly, play dice,
guess fingers. Once a girl rises and dances briefly
with her shoulders, hips, and belly, wtihout moving
her feet. The flute player plays the first phrase and
then two voices, at the interval of a fifth, with the
higher an octave under the very high flute, sing the
first Delphic Hymn, very high and faint, in Greek:

En klyta megapolis
Atthis euchaieisi
Pheroploio naiousa
Tritoonidos dapedon
Athrauston. Hagiois

De bomoioisin Haphaistos
Ai eithei neon
Merataouron.
Homouou de nin Araps
Atmos es Olympon
Anakidnatai. Liau
De lotoos bremon
Aeioloiois melesin
Odaan krekei. Chrysea
D'adythrous kitharis
Hymnoisin anamelpetai.

*As the song is ending, Kalliope enters, sees the body
of Demetrios, goes slowly and stands above it, be-
tween the bodies of Hermaios and Tarakaia, facing
the audience, as if waiting. The flute player starts a
few notes. Menander enters as if to the music. The
flute stops and Menander stops at the far right and
forward, facing Kalliope.*

II Chorus
Put the wineskin near the fire.

Ice is forming on its mouth.

Is this all?

This is the end.

I Chorus
Parallel lines meet sooner
Than some think.

KALLIOPE

I expected you.
In fact I was searching for you.

I CHORUS

Only those who were enemies
In former lives meet in this one.

MENANDER

How did you know that I had come?

KALLIOPE

Do you think you are the only
One who can decipher his fate?
I am closer to you than the
Veins of your throat. I knew you when
You were hovering over the grave
Of my womb. Why are you waiting?
Did you draw that sword to hunt owls?

MENANDER

I do not dare to take vengeance. . . .
I CHORUS

. . . If I should dare to
Lay my hand on a grain of
Sand by way of vengeance, I would
Punish the already punished.
If there are gods, I cannot act
For them.

KALLIOPE

Sometimes, my dear son, it
Is wise to propitiate
The idol and ignore the god.
Gods are impassive but idols
Are irritable and vindictive.
You need not fear the consequence,
Action is cancelled by action.

I CHORUS

Each man has a ghostly double,
When he does a good deed, his twin
Does an evil one, when he sins
The double does a good deed.

The dove devours her prey, the
Vulture sings like the nightingale.

KALLIOPE

Are you still afraid of the dark?

MENANDER

No. The only thing I fear in the dark
Is my reflexion in a mirror.

KALLIOPE

And I, the heart's darkness, the love
Of parent for child. You do not know,
As I know, your helplessness.
Your sword moves through a thousand years
And drags your hand and your immobile
Heart with it. It will cut this hinge

187

Between light and dark, and nothing
You can do will stop its course. No.
Your task is very easy.

She bares her breasts.

It
Takes time for blood to become milk.
It's easy to turn milk to blood.

Menander starts walking slowly towards her, moving to the words of the First Chorus. His sword drops lower with each step.

I CHORUS

It is necessary that things
Should pass away into that from
Which they were born.

All things must pay
To each other the penalties
And compensation for all the
Inequalities wrought by time.

II CHORUS

The gates are on fire.

There are
Torches coming up the road.

KALLIOPE

Hurry. The time is almost full.

I CHORUS

The rainbows flow on forever.

Another virgin twists in birth.

The key turns in the lock.

The star
Crosses the zenith.

The child comes
Forth like light through glass.

Another
God is nailed upon the heavens.

Lost on the poisonous waves
Of an untraversable sea,

We meet and touch and pass on,
As log meets log in mid-ocean.

II CHORUS
The Huns!

The Huns!

*Bass horns, counterbassoons and/or bass viols sound
their lowest notes off stage. This deep drone con-
tinues till the end of the play.*

*Menander runs with uplifted sword toward the edge
of the cliff on the left rear of the stage. As he passes
the center, Kalliope throws herself from between
the catafalques onto his sword, and falls back, her
head on the step, at the feet of Demetrios, diag-
onally between Hermaios and Tarakaia. Berenike
runs in, sees the dead queen, pulls the sword from
her body, starts to lift it over her head. Menander*

takes it from her and gives it to the First Chorus, to the beggar, who gives him his bowl in exchange. The prostitute gives her jewels to Berenike, who gives her Tarakaia's ring. The beggar and prostitute step behind the center screen and Menander and Berenike take their places and assume their attitudes. The Second Chorus cease to act, and assume the formal positions of musicians unconcerned with the events of the stage. The Huns rush on and dance a wild, acrobatic military dance while the impassive figures of the new First Chorus watch them.

New Directions Paperbooks

Walter Abish, *Alphabetical Africa*. NDP375.
Ilangô Adigal, *Shilappadikaram*. NDP162.
Brother Antoninus, *The Residual Years*. NDP263.
Guillaume Apollinaire, *Selected Writings.†* NDP310.
Djuna Barnes, *Nightwood*. NDP98.
Charles Baudelaire, *Flowers of Evil.†* NDP71.
Paris Spleen. NDP294.
Gottfried Benn, *Primal Vision*. NDP322.
Eric Bentley, *Bernard Shaw*. NDP59.
Wolfgang Borchert, *The Man Outside*. NDP319.
Jorge Luis Borges, *Labyrinths*. NDP186.
Jean-François Bory, *Once Again*. NDP256.
Kay Boyle, *Thirty Stories*. NDP62.
E. Brock, *Invisibility Is The Art of Survival*. NDP342.
The Portraits & The Poses. NDP360.
W. Bronk, *The World, the Worldless*. NDP157.
Buddha, *The Dhammapada*. NDP188.
Hayden Carruth, *For You*. NDP298.
From Snow and Rock, from Chaos. NDP349.
Louis-Ferdinand Céline,
Death on the Installment Plan. NDP330.
Guignol's Band. NDP278.
Journey to the End of the Night. NDP84.
Blaise Cendrars, *Selected Writings.†* NDP203.
B-c. Chatterjee, *Krishnakanta's Will*. NDP120.
Jean Cocteau, *The Holy Terrors*. NDP212.
The Infernal Machine. NDP235.
M. Cohen, *Monday Rhetoric*. NDP352.
Cid Corman, *Livingdying*. NDP289.
Sun Rock Man. NDP318.
Gregory Corso, *Elegiac Feelings American*. NDP299.
Long Live Man. NDP127.
Happy Birthday of Death. NDP86.
Edward Dahlberg, *Reader*. NDP246.
Because I Was Flesh. NDP227.
David Daiches, *Virginia Woolf*. (Revised) NDP96.
Osamu Dazai, *The Setting Sun*. NDP258.
No Longer Human. NDP357.
Coleman Dowell, *Mrs. October Was Here*. NDP368.
Robert Duncan, *Roots and Branches*. NDP275.
Bending the Bow. NDP255.
The Opening of the Field. NDP356.
Richard Eberhart, *Selected Poems*. NDP198.
Russell Edson, *The Very Thing That Happens*. NDP137.
Wm. Empson, *7 Types of Ambiguity*. NDP204.
Some Versions of Pastoral. NDP92.
Wm. Everson, *The Residual Years*. NDP263.
Man-Fate. NDP369.
Lawrence Ferlinghetti, *Her*. NDP88.
Back Roads to Far Places. NDP312.
A Coney Island of the Mind. NDP74.
The Mexican Night. NDP300.
Open Eye, Open Heart. NDP361.
Routines. NDP187.
The Secret Meaning of Things. NDP268.
Starting from San Francisco. NDP 220.
Tyrannus Nix?. NDP288.
Ronald Firbank, *Two Novels*. NDP128.
Dudley Fitts,
Poems from the Greek Anthology. NDP60.
F. Scott Fitzgerald, *The Crack-up*. NDP54.
Robert Fitzgerald, *Spring Shade: Poems 1931-1970*. NDP311.
Gustave Flaubert,
Bouvard and Pécuchet. NDP328.
The Dictionary of Accepted Ideas. NDP230.
M. K. Gandhi, *Gandhi on Non-Violence*. (ed. Thomas Merton) NDP197.
André Gide, *Dostoevsky*. NDP100.
Goethe, *Faust*, Part I. (MacIntyre translation) NDP70.

Albert J. Guerard, *Thomas Hardy*. NDP185.
Guillevic, *Selected Poems*. NDP279.
Henry Hatfield, *Goethe*. NDP136.
Thomas Mann. (Revised Edition) NDP101.
John Hawkes, *The Cannibal*. NDP123.
The Lime Twig. NDP95.
Second Skin. NDP146.
The Beetle Leg. NDP239.
The Blood Oranges. NDP338.
The Innocent Party. NDP238.
Lunar Landscapes. NDP274.
A. Hayes, *A Wreath of Christmas Poems*. NDP347.
H.D., *Hermetic Definition*. NDP343.
Trilogy. NDP362.
Hermann Hesse, *Siddhartha*. NDP65.
Christopher Isherwood, *The Berlin Stories*. NDP134.
Gustav Janouch,
Conversations With Kafka. NDP313.
Alfred Jarry, *Ubu Roi*. NDP105.
Robinson Jeffers, *Cawdor and Medea*. NDP293.
James Joyce, *Stephen Hero*. NDP133.
James Joyce/Finnegans Wake. NDP331.
Franz Kafka, *Amerika*. NDP117.
Bob Kaufman,
Solitudes Crowded with Loneliness. NDP199.
Hugh Kenner, *Wyndham Lewis*. NDP167.
Kenyon Critics, *Gerard Manley Hopkins*. NDP355.
P. Lal, translator, *Great Sanskrit Plays*. NDP142.
Tommaso Landolfi,
Gogol's Wife and Other Stories. NDP155.
Lautréamont, *Maldoror*. NDP207.
Denise Levertov, *Footprints*. NDP344.
The Jacob's Ladder. NDP112.
The Poet in the World. NDP363.
O Taste and See. NDP149.
Relearning the Alphabet. NDP290.
The Sorrow Dance. NDP222.
To Stay Alive. NDP325.
With Eyes at the Back of Our Heads. NDP229.
Harry Levin, *James Joyce*. NDP87.
García Lorca, *Selected Poems.†* NDP114.
Three Tragedies. NDP52.
Five Plays. NDP232.
Michael McClure, *September Blackberries*. NDP370.
Carson McCullers, *The Member of the Wedding*. (Playscript) NDP153.
Thomas Merton, *Cables to the Ace*. NDP252.
Emblems of a Season of Fury. NDP140.
Gandhi on Non-Violence. NDP197.
The Geography of Lograire. NDP283.
New Seeds of Contemplation. NDP337.
Raids on the Unspeakable. NDP213.
Selected Poems. NDP85.
The Way of Chuang Tzu. NDP276.
The Wisdom of the Desert. NDP295.
Zen and the Birds of Appetite. NDP261.
Henri Michaux, *Selected Writings.†* NDP264.
Henry Miller, *The Air-Conditioned Nightmare*. NDP302.
Big Sur & The Oranges of Hieronymus Bosch. NDP161.
The Books in My Life. NDP280.
The Colossus of Maroussi. NDP75.
The Cosmological Eye. NDP109.
Henry Miller on Writing. NDP151.
The Henry Miller Reader. NDP269.
Remember to Remember. NDP111.
Stand Still Like the Hummingbird. NDP236.
The Time of the Assassins. NDP115.
The Wisdom of the Heart. NDP94.
Y. Mishima, *Death in Midsummer*. NDP215.
Confessions of a Mask. NDP253.
Eugenio Montale, *Selected Poems.†* NDP193.

Complete descriptive catalog available free on request from
New Directions, 333 Sixth Avenue, New York 10014.   † Bilingual.